GW00372829

Antiques are flourishing as never before; records are constantly being broken in the sale rooms, and for antiques recession has never existed. But there are antiques and antiques; there are pseudo-antiques, and there is rubbish masquerading as antiques. The newcomer can come to grief, and needs a friendly guide to help him or her through the minefield. This book aims to be such a guide – what to buy, what not to buy, where to buy, and what to look for. The author takes a sharp look at some of the more familiar antiques, and explores the possibility of the more novel collectables, such as samplers and Victorian glass.

There is a valuable chapter on how the antique trade works, which rids it of some of the mystery that has gathered around it. The notorious dealers' ring is explained, and shown not to be so terrible as outsiders suppose. There is also a list of antique markets, invaluable to holidaymakers and those in an unfamiliar part of the country.

But above all this book takes a refreshing look at the things people collect. One collects antiques for pleasure; but there is nothing wrong in making money from them, too.

Widen Your Horizons with this series

Remember that we cater for all interests. See for yourself with our varied list of titles.

Places to see

Scottish Islands – Tom Weir
Dartmoor – Crispin Gill

Leisure activities

Good Photography Made Easy – Derek Watkins
Cine Photography Made Easy – Derek Watkins
Looking at Churches – David Bowen
Railways for Pleasure – Geoffrey Body
Brass and Other Rubbings – Emma Wood
Wine and Beer Making – Derek Watkins

Sporting

The Art of Good Shooting – J. E. M. Ruffer
Archery for All – Daniel Roberts
Rowing for Everyone – Christopher Chant
Sea Fishing for Fun – Alan Wrangles and Jack P. Tupper

Holidays

Pony Trekking – Edward Hart
Inland Waterways – Charles Hadfield

The Antique-Hunter's Handbook

Ronald Rawlings

David & Charles

Newton Abbot   London   North Pomfret (Vt)   Vancouver

British Library Cataloguing in Publication Data

Rawlings, Ronald
    The antique-hunter's handbook. – (David & Charles leisure and travel series).
    1. Art objects – Collectors and collecting
    I. Title   II. Series
    745.1   NK1125

    ISBN 0-7153-7578-4

Typeset by Tradespools Limited, Frome
and printed in Great Britain by
Redwood Burn Limited, Trowbridge & Esher
for David & Charles (Publishers) Limited
Brunel House Newton Abbot Devon

Published in the United States of America
by David & Charles Inc
North Pomfret Vermont 05053 USA

Published in Canada
by Douglas David & Charles Limited
1875 Welch Street North Vancouver BC

Contents

List of illustrations

1 Finding out about Antiques

There is no substitute for looking at things, and if possible handling them. The best place to handle antiques is in an antique shop. Most antiques will not come to pieces in your hands. The best kind of antique shop is one where you have bought something; a dealer is not an advice bureau, as is so often thought, but if you have bought something and there appears to be every chance of your buying something else there will be no objection to your handling items and asking questions about them.

It is instructive to go to museums and compare what they have there with the same sort of thing in antique shops. A piece of porcelain worth £1,000 may at first glance look like something very similar priced at £10 in an antique shop. If, with the best will in the world, you can see no difference after a long scrutiny steer clear of porcelain.

Television programmes have brought antiques to the multitude, and no one would begrudge a viewer the delight of seeing a Sheraton table whisked before his very eyes. But even the most respectable antique programme is entertainment, not instruction. Do not be jollied along into believing that your grannie's chamber-pot is worth £30. At the other end of the scale, hundreds of dealers would have liked to buy several items 'going for a song' at the experts' valuations.

The numerous price guides available can provide useful hints, but they are not Bibles. They do not compare with Glass's guide as used by the motor trade to determine dealers' prices for second-hand cars. The compilers rely on auction records, not always infallible indications of *real* supply and demand. The main disadvantage of price guides is that they so rapidly become out of date, even though Lyle's excellent series is newly updated every year. It is no secret that most dealers have a copy of Lyle's guide tucked away in their desk, and it must be true that Lyle's initiate some price levels rather than merely record them.

Books, of course, are the most convenient way of studying antiques, and are usually reliable. No publishers let an idiot loose on a book that will cost at least two thousand pounds to produce.

Magazines, even antique magazines, are less to be recommended; many articles are downright misleading, and in one issue of a well-known magazine I counted twelve errors of fact. Chat articles in the popular press can be even worse, though the antique pages in the superior women's magazines are usually excellent.

Fellow collectors are, of course, the best source of genuine knowledge – if they tell you what you want to know, though enthusiasm is apt to rise over self-interest.

Above all, frequent auctions, and if necessary be one of those people in the front row who take down prices without ever buying a thing. It is good fun to view the auction, and jot down the prices you anticipate the articles will fetch. And at auctions you will be able to handle anything you see, except perhaps the auctioneer's lady clerk. The silver and small valuables will be locked away in a cabinet. Ask the porter to let you see them, and prod around a bit. No porter has yet been born who will refuse to open a jewellery cabinet.

There is no incentive more compelling than the delight in buying something and selling it at a profit. Newcomers to antiques often find it easier to sell through a sale room than privately; the personal touch can initially be embarrassing. But choose your sale room carefully. There *are* snooty auction rooms with snooty young men and women behind the desk, and before you put items into an auction it is a good idea to spy out the ground. You would not want to put a priceless heirloom into a sale room filled with cookers and vacuum cleaners, or vice versa.

2 How the Antique Trade Works

Antique dealers, like antiques, come in all shapes and sizes, but no matter who they are their aim is to buy something and sell it at a profit. This may seem glaringly obvious, but it is a point worth remembering (and one sometimes forgotten by the dealers themselves). A dealer who does not sell his stock is either playing at being a dealer or goes out of business.

An antique dealer buys from a variety of sources.

Auctions

These vary from cottage sales where the most delectable item might well be a three-piece suite to Sotheby's, Christie's, and Phillips', the three giants. The auctioneer makes his money by charging commission (usually from 10 to 15 per cent). This once applied to the seller only, but many auctioneers now charge the buyer as well. Auctioneering is thus a profitable business. Although a prospective buyer has the opportunity to examine anything in the sale room, he has to make a spot decision when it comes to the crunch. A dealer usually marks his catalogue with the prices he or she is willing to pay, but occasionally the most prudent go wild and overbid.

A private buyer can outbid a dealer simply because he does not have to think about making a profit. Sometimes at an auction a private buyer might think an item has been sold much too cheaply; but this is misleading. It merely means that the 'ring' is in operation. The ring is an agreement between dealers not to bid against each other. They appoint a spokesman, who buys the item at the cheapest possible price. It is then auctioned off later in private at the 'knock-out', and the difference between the price obtained at auction and in the knock-out is divided between the members of the ring. The dealers' ring is illegal but no way has been found to prevent it operating. At smaller auctions, *every* worthwhile item will be bought by the ring. The person who suffers most is the vendor, and anybody putting goods into auction should make

11

certain that a sensible reserve is placed on them, so that they cannot be sold too cheaply.

A private buyer *can* compete with the ring, but if he or she is too persistent the ring will run the price up. This means that the private buyer will pay more than was anticipated (very easy to do in the excitement of a sale room). It is known for private 'punters' to watch a certain successful dealer, and buy the item bidded for when the dealer drops out, reckoning, logically enough, that by spending two or three pounds more than the dealer a bargain has been obtained. These private buyers are known as 'followers' and, once spotted, they are very vulnerable. The dealer *knows* that he can carry on, and the follower will still top him; the dealer can thus force the follower to overpay on every item.

A large proportion of all goods in a regular auction (as opposed to a house auction) are put in by dealers, who reckon that they can get more there than in their shops. Often they are stale items that have been around a long time. A new environment often sells things, even to buyers who have seen the self-same goods in the vendor's shop.

Call-outs

A call-out is a private person who goes to a dealer's shop or replies to an advertisement (straight-forward or cunning as the case may be), offering to sell the dealer something. Many antique dealers keep shops open for this, and this only. There is always the chance of buying something extremely valuable, something not on the market before, something not seen by any knowledgeable person. A dealer who has any sense gives a fair price for any goods offered. A low price might mean the vendor going elsewhere and someone else making the profit, or the vendor going elsewhere for any future transactions. On the other hand, a fair price means that the dealer may get custom not only from that person, but by word of mouth from friends and acquaintances of a satisfied customer.

A dealer can come unstuck by buying from this source. In his desperation to get the goods offered to him, he may overpay; he may be offered something he does not know anything about, and grossly overpay. And he can buy something hot, stolen, and dangerous to know. He can also be conned by a dealer masquerading as a private seller, and presented with a 'dog', a 'mock-up', or a 'moody' (all terms indicating an item about which there is something suspect).

Many people are more aware of antiques and their values than was once the case, and often expect more than they are offered. Many of them go window-shopping, looking at prices, and expect very nearly the same for their own items; often they assume that dealers work on a 10 per cent profit margin, as if they were selling packets of cigarettes.

Other Dealers

An immense amount of business takes place between dealers, and the private trade is, on the whole, of minor significance. This may seem surprising, for ultimately the antique must end in the hands of a person who owns it for its own sake. There are many dealers who only deal with the trade, and whose shops serve no purpose other than to store goods. Obviously the more affluent dealers buy from their less fortunate colleagues, though much of the business is carried out between dealers on the same footing, hoping that an item in someone else's shop will sell in theirs at a rather higher price. Expertise comes in here. A dealer in silver may not care much for pictures, and although most dealers buy anything that comes their way they will happily part with something they do not know anything about at a small profit. For instance, a coin dealer may buy a half-sovereign at five pounds, he would not sell it for under twenty-five pounds. But he may buy a picture for five pounds, and sell it for eight (a usual 'mark-up') even though it may be worth a hundred to a dealer who knows about paintings.

The aim of dealers selling to each other is to 'leave something in it' for both to make a comfortable profit. This keeps stock moving in the hope that eventually it will go outside the area, perhaps to London and the expensive end of the market, or via a shipper, overseas. The shippers are the big dealers; they operate at both ends of the antique spectrum, from articles that hardly qualify as antiques such as gate-leg tables of the 1920s and 1930s to bureaux-bookcases in the £1,500–£2,000 range. The shippers operate on a fairly small profit margin (10 to 20 per cent) and rely on a huge turnover for their success (often of the order of £50,000 a week).

Many dealers make their living selling to the shippers; they are known as 'runners'.

The shippers do not have shops, and never deal with the general public, though the trade can often buy from them, especially the more out of the way items which have not yet found a ready market abroad. These exporters have been largely responsible for the denudation of Victoriana, favoured a few years ago by the Australians and the Americans and now bought up by the Europeans, who will buy anything with a few knobs on. When the British economy recovers there is no question that it will all be bought back. The wholesale export of Victoriana, especially Victorian furniture, has made even indifferent and sometimes downright shoddy items of the period inordinately over-priced, and this should be borne in mind when buying furnishing pieces (though there are exceptions to prove the rule – ebonized furniture remains, as it has done for twenty years, undervalued).

Jumble Sales

For many years jumble sales were a happy hunting ground for antique dealers, but with growing public awareness of the value of oddments jumble sales are now less interesting and consist largely of clothes. There *are* worthwhile items amongst the junk, but not very often, and most dealers do not find it worth their while to chase around the church halls, leaving the chore to market-stall holders or junk dealers for whom a bucket or a tin of emulsion paint spells twenty pence or so.

Markets

These range from village markets with the accent on fruit and veg to the antique markets which are really mini-antique shops arranged under one roof or in one area (such as the Portobello Road or Camden Passage, Islington). Most village markets have bric-à-brac stalls, and dealers will keep an eye on these, because market traders work very hard for little reward and can sometimes find things of value in the course of their travels. However, as most market traders do different markets on different days it is a question of first come, first served. Markets start early, and if there are any startling bargains going it is usually before 8 am. The Bermondsey antique market, known as the Caledonian though it moved from north London many years ago, becomes active soon after midnight on Thursdays. Markets are the most interesting places for the public and the trade to buy at. In the first place, the stall-holder is anxious to sell, for most markets fold up at about 1 pm, and as it is hard work a market trader likes to feel that his vigil is worthwhile. At the high-class antique markets, such as the Antique Supermarket behind Selfridges or Antiquarius in the King's Road, prices are no cheaper than in antique shops, but at the antique markets that have proliferated throughout Britain over the last ten years they often are. The market trader, because of low overheads, can afford to let things go cheaply.

The street market at its best – the rough end of Portobello Road

Junk Dealers

Everyone loves a good honest junk shop, and it is sad that there are fewer of them about. Junk by definition is cheap, and although in days gone by junk dealers could rub along on next to nothing, escalating rates and prohibitive rents have forced most of them to give up. The more adventurous ones have graduated into antiques, but for many times have proved too hard. Junk dealers served as useful middle men, clearing houses, selling the poor stuff themselves or to market traders, dumping the absolute rubbish, and selling the reasonable items to antique dealers. Comparable with the junk dealers were the rag-and-bone men, who have also been hit by changed conditions. High-rise flats and modern housing estates do not encourage the hoarding of junk, unlike the decrepit terrace houses and slums that preceded them. The rag-and-bone man provided an invaluable service, removing not only old stoves from houses but also bringing a wealth of more saleable objects on to the market. He began to decline when the lack of stabling in the big cities forced him to exchange his pony (always pony, never horse) for a van. The rag-and-bone man has been replaced by the 'totter', who deals in anything that will make money, from rags, scrap metal, and bits and pieces to antiques. Nothing is too menial for him, from scrabbling around the municipal tip to prowling through derelict houses in the hope of finding something of value.

Knockers

A 'knocker' is a person who goes from door to door trying to buy goods. He can be educated and knowledgeable and driving a Volvo, or he can be rough, not averse to bullying little old ladies ('biddies') or slipping the odd silver spoon into his pocket. Knockers build up connections with certain dealers, but their most certain outlet is the shipper who will usually buy the van-load, taking the good with the bad. The most energetic knockers are the 'tinkers' who operate from their caravans and encampments and who are often surprisingly knowledgeable. The tinkers go out in groups and saturate an area. They deal only in cash, and it is not unusual to see a tinker with a 'wad' of two thousand pounds or more.

House Clearances

Some dealers advertise that they clear houses. This might seem an odd pursuit, but it can be profitable. House clearances usually occur after a death, especially the death of an elderly person in whom no one is particularly interested. A dealer offers a price for the contents of a house, and undertakes to remove everything from it. Everything means everything, from soiled bed-linen to empty cardboard boxes, and it can be an unpleasant and arduous task, so much so that many dealers would rather miss out on house clearances, especially elderly and finicky dealers. If they do put in a price it is to 'pull' a few choice items, subcontracting the dirty work to someone else. A few of the more lowly dealers have permanent arrangements with more affluent dealers, so that they have the dross from any clearance, selling it in a garage or a barn for small amounts; dealers sometimes do a deal with executors and the like so that if any house clearance comes up they have first pick.

Antique Fairs

These have become very fashionable over the last ten years, and are really upgraded antique markets, with a charge for public admission. Such a charge is puzzling, if not actually insane. The idea of antique fairs stems from the continent, which lacks the immense variety of antique shops that form part of the British scene. It is customary to limit items on show in an antique fair, often by date. This is in itself ludicrous, because items of the 1950s now appear for sale at Sotheby's. Of even more recent vintage is the collectors' fair, containing such articles as postcards, bookmarks, posters, and music-covers.

Dealers with shops often find it worth their while to have a stall in an antiques fair at £15–£20 a day. A concentration of dealers *does* bring in the buying public. Dealers welcome new dealers into their town; it is one sphere where competition is appreciated. A serious buyer with limited time will think twice about visiting a place where there is only one antique shop. The presence of three or four often tips the balance.

These are the basic supply sources of the antique dealers. Sometimes the dealer will bring things from his own house for resale, and often he will put something in his shop on a sale or return basis, especially if it is an expensive piece or an item in which he has little confidence. It is usual for a vendor to specify an acceptable price, and the dealer adds his percentage. Accepting items on sale or return is a good way of building up stock without paying out cash.

The private buyer interested in antiques for themselves or as profitable investments cannot always get at the primary sources, though in most cases he or she can compete on equal terms with the dealers. Private buyers are always welcomed at antique fairs, markets, and in most antique shops, except those marked 'Trade Only' which can mean just that and which are shunned by many dealers because of the open contempt it shows for the private buyer. Rudeness is abominable anywhere, and self-destructive when applied to the great British tradition of buying and selling.

Dealers are often obliged to buy objects which do not interest them to make money, but a collector is not. It is unrewarding and ill-advised to buy certain kinds of antique purely for their money-making possibilities. A collector should buy what interests or stirs him or her. In this way, it is difficult not to become at least a mini-expert, and knowledge breeds confidence. A serious collector becomes, almost without realizing it, a dealer, for as discrimination comes in so does the collector jettison early acquisitions in favour of more laudable specimens. In selling off unwanted pieces the collector will naturally try to get more than he paid for them.

A collector will have an edge on a dealer who is not a specialist; even the most successful and acute dealer has gaps in his knowledge, and must expect to have this deficiency traded upon by people who know more than he does. This will not mean that he will sell goods at a loss, but it will mean that he will sell items he does not reckon at less than their going rate – the going rate being determined by the laws of supply and demand for that particular item, be it a shaving-mug, a silk bookmark, or a Louis Wain postcard, all collectable pieces.

The kind of collecting one does depends, quite simply, on the kind of money available. It is fruitless for a person with a hundred pounds to specialize in, say, Bow china; but a person with a hundred pounds could build up a definitive collection of shaving-mugs. For rich collectors there are specialist dealers. They can be seen in the fashionable areas of London with perhaps a dozen items in their windows. The important thing about specialist dealers is that they furnish a guarantee by their mere existence. A dealer in fine furniture is on the downward slope if he sells a Georgian table which is not 'right'. The reputation of these favoured few depends on their giving value for money – even if the money is thousands of pounds per item rather than twenty.

For collectors less well endowed the type of shops to look for are those containing an interesting general stock with a wide price range. A small stock does not mean that the shop is not worth investigating; it may mean that the owner has a good turn-over and happens to be running low in goods. But it can also mean that the dealer has run short of buying capital, and is patiently sitting on what goods he has left, goods that may have been in the shop months or years. A good clue is the amount of dust the items have gathered; an even better clue is a dog-eared price label.

Some dealers do not price their goods. This is very tiresome as it means that he or she is making an assessment of the customer, working out how much profit can be made. Much the same applies to the use of a code. Most dealers' codes are complex and unbreak-able, often the initial letters of some phrase. The more naive dealers use A = 1, B = 2, C = 3, etc. The use of a code may be seen as needlessly obscurantist, but it does serve a purpose. It stops browsers using an antique shop as a free price guide to their own possessions. Where prices are clearly marked there is often another figure in the corner of the label, sometimes prefaced by the letter 'T'. This is the trade price, or the trade discount. The private collector should bear the trade price in mind when an article is considered. It does not matter to the dealer whether he sells to a private customer or another dealer. The display of a trade price is a kind of game. Dealers expect to have something knocked off, and if they see T − 2 (the stated price less £2) they are happy. Some brave dealers proudly announce that they do not give a trade price to anybody, but this is cutting off their noses to spite their faces.

Many dealers of the middle range make a feature of tempting offers such as a 20p basket, just as in the old days a bookseller had a threepenny box. Few can resist going through a 20p basket, even seasoned veterans of the antique game. In a sense, the 20p basket is a loss leader, tempting people to venture further into the shop and look around. If more people looked in antique shops, rather than peered through the windows as if at an aquarium, they would find things that were amazingly cheap. A modern blue-and-white teacup and saucer costs £1.50; so does a Victorian Copeland blue-and-white teacup and saucer. Both serve the same purpose, and which is better, which will increase in value? It is a question to which there is only one answer.

Antiques are not only fit to be put on a shelf, but also to be used. A pretty 1930s tea-service will in all probability cost less than a humdrum china tea-service from a department store; a handsome Victorian chest-of-drawers will certainly cost a good deal less than something made yesterday. And why buy a modern custom-built ash tray when one can pick up a pretty Victorian dish for 50p?

Some collectors are frightened of auctions, fearing that by twitching or blowing their noses they will be lumbered with some piece of monumental rubbish. There is no possible chance of this. Auctioneers are professionals; it is their business to know who is bidding. Most of the regular buyers will be known to them, and an auction pattern soon emerges. If there is any ambiguity the auctioneer will simply ask: 'Are you bidding, sir?' (or madam). Once the auctioneer has established the existence of a new bidder he will keep an eye on him or her. And then the business of the brusque nod of the head can come in. This is not an affectation. By bidding surreptitiously the buyer can keep his intentions quiet from other bidders. To get in a bid one does not have to go into contortions or madly wave a catalogue; a brisk flip of the catalogue or a raised finger will catch the auctioneer's eye. And if he does not see you and seems to want to ignore you, don't be afraid to make your presence known by calling out. There are good auctioneers and there are slapdash auctioneers; but you are not there for your health, and there is no need to feel embarrassment for pulling the auctioneer up for negligence.

Too strenuous haggling is not advised, either in shops or at markets. You are not in a Turkish bazaar. If you are not prepared to pay the price on the label it is quite in order to suggest a price rather less — rather less, but not ridiculously less. If an object is priced at £20 it is silly to offer £8 for it, though some people do.

3   Collectable Antiques

In selecting categories of collectable antiques there is always the problem of what to leave out. I have tried to cover a wide spectrum. Impossible to leave out furniture or porcelain, of course, but where obvious subjects have been selected I have tried to take a new and I hope refreshing line. In 'fringe' antiques I have dealt with items that are little known or little valued, but always I have kept in mind the question of availability. And I am not writing for millionaires or those with a few thousand pounds burning a hole in the pocket. So readers will look in vain for articles on singing birds, medieval icons, or the work of Fabergé. These *have* turned up in unlikely places, and if the reader happens to strike lucky I will be the first to offer congratulations. But I do not hold great hopes of it.

Art Deco

Art Deco (sometimes left in its French form *art déco*) is a name for the decorative arts of the 1920s and 1930s, and covers a multitude of objects. Its appeal is both nostalgic and aesthetic. Art Deco was presented to the world in a Paris exhibition in 1925. The accent was on streamlining, modernism, and away with the hangovers of Victoriana and Edwardiana, but Art Deco covers not only modernism but quaint simplicity and it is difficult to say what did *not* influence it.

There is an immense amount of Art Deco about; much of it is good, much of it is awful, but if it reflects the period it is usually interesting, even the self-conscious 'modernistic' mirrors and chain-store china. Older readers will be able to pick out Art Deco without knowing why; it will simply remind them of younger days. Besides streamlining everything, there was a delight in putting utilitarian things in a novel context. So we get teapots shaped like racing-cars, cigarette lighters hidden inside a chrome barman, and grandfather clocks (properly called long-case clocks) disguising a cocktail cabinet. Among the influences that make Art Deco so recognizable was Aztec art, especially the stepped shapes of Aztec temples which can be seen in wireless sets and clocks of the period. The 1920s and particularly the 1930s liked hard-looking stone of the kind used by the Aztecs, such as rock crystal, obsidian (a natural glass) and onyx. Chrome was loved, and so were exotic combinations, a favourite being ivory and bronze for statues and decorative pieces. Western films had an important effect on things in the home, and ideas taken from the Red Indians made a somewhat odd contribution to soft furnishing design.

The ancient Egyptians also influenced Art Deco. The opening of Tutankhamen's tomb in 1922 created quite an industry in Egyptiana, and we see its effect in jewellery, furniture, and buildings, particularly cinemas. Egyptian motifs merged very well with the Aztec notions, and with the other decorative titbits that ornamented everything that could be ornamented – the electric zigzag, the sunray, or the streamlined dog. There was a lot of adventure among the designers. They did not see why a cup should not be square with triangular handles, or why something that looked like a tennis-ball should not splay open to reveal a cigarette-lighter. They did not see why a carpet should not have bright geometric patterns that almost trip you up. They did not see why they should not use the new plastics in green, orange, and purple, instead of the dull and respectable Bakelite (a trade name originally, but later used to describe anything of brown plastic).

The diversity of Art Deco is almost unbelievable, and so are the prices asked, anything from £1 to £20 *for the same article*. Pretty bits of china can be picked up from 20p, Art Deco compacts, usually beautifully made, range from £1 apiece, and Art Deco cigarette boxes, either for the pocket or table models, from hardly more. Art Deco furniture, particularly French furniture, can be expensive, especially if it leans towards the stark simplicity of what was known as functionalism (a chair does not have to be comfortable, only sittable in). The bulbous armchairs and somewhat flashy sideboards and tables are cheap, *and* very well made.

Qualities to look for in Art Deco are individuality and craftsmanship. The men and women involved in the decorative arts had access to a wealth of technical aids, and although there are fine one-offs much of the material one comes across in the lower price ranges was commercial, made in quantity. This does not mean it was shoddy; the standard of what is known in the manufacturing industries as 'quality control' was high.

Art Nouveau

Art nouveau flourished from about 1890 to 1910, tapering off just before World War I and timidly revived in the early 1920s. *Art nouveau* was a reaction against stodginess and convention, and if possible avoided using straight lines. It was curvaceous, and drew inspiration from plant forms, such as the lily and the tulip. The designers loved odd shapes, whether they were creating buildings, pottery, or the more mundane things about the home such as tables and chairs, door-knockers, furniture-handles, and cutlery. *Art nouveau* rediscovered pewter, and there was hardly a house in middle-class England which did not have some article or other made from this neglected alloy; the whole movement reflected a delight in eccentricity.

It was a world-wide movement, and was immensely influential in the United States and France. *Art nouveau* in Britain was idiosyncratic rather than stylish, and was soundly attacked by the Establishment. The objects reminded one celebrated artist of 'exploded dum-dum bullets'; Walter Crane thought it a 'strange decorative disease'. However, many of the characteristics of Walter Crane's work were also found in *art nouveau*, especially the influence of Japanese art.

Two of the most important names in *art nouveau* are Louis Tiffany, son of an American jeweller, whose glass lamp-shades are in the four-figure league, and Émile Gallé whose odd-shaped glassware provided an inspiration to both workers in glass and potters. Besides glass and pewter, *art nouveau* designers rediscovered beaten copper, and articles in this material are not hard to come by at a reasonable cost. They include mirror-surrounds, trays of all shapes and sizes, boxes, and plaques.

Comparable with Tiffany and Gallé was René Lalique, who used the *art nouveau* forms for his jewellery. After World War I he turned his attention to glass, and in both these spheres he is much collected. The ordinary collector can, of course, look out for signed *art nouveau* but the great majority of the items he is likely to come across in his travels are anonymous. The smaller pieces are

Art nouveau at its lightest — an illustration by Raphael Kirchner (*Victoria & Albert Museum*)

still inexpensive, but if it is in metal, the bigger the thing the more expensive. The French of this period went in for drawing-room sculpture in this style.

It is easy enough to get the feel of typical *art nouveau*, but along with the swirly plant-like forms there was an interest in the ungainly-chunky look, derived from the Arts and Crafts Movement. The idea was to give the appearance of being hand-made, even if it was not. If you like, the chunky look is a masculine counterpart to the more feminine side of *art nouveau*. There is no danger of getting confused with heavy Victoriana, particularly Victorian furniture; the Victorians thought their furniture was sturdy when it was merely being pompous.

Art nouveau is not often pompous; it can be frivolous, quaint, and, above all, arty and affected, but for those who take the trouble to get to know it it can be endearing. It accompanied an age of freedom and optimism. Smaller items that have increased in value are postcards, especially those designed by Mucha, hatpins, curiously shaped hair-combs, and jewellery. The elongations and distortions that become perverse in furniture have a charm when transferred to the miniature form.

The Arts and Crafts Movement

The Arts and Crafts Movement was a self-conscious rebellion against industrialization, and its leaders such as John Ruskin and William Morris envisaged an idealistic state where everyone worked at what they liked doing. Furniture, pots and pans, wallpaper, and everything that served to decorate or equip a house would be created with love and affection. Factories would give way to crafts workshops, and Britain would be a conglomeration of High Wycombes (for a long time the centre of the chair-making industry).

It did not work out like that. At the lowest level, only factories could fill the demand of a rich consumer society. And people did not particularly want hand-made articles when there was a serviceable alternative at a tenth of the price. The leading Arts and Crafts firm was Morris, Marshall, Faulkner & Co., established in 1861, first producing ecclesiastical items, later furniture, glass, metalware and tiles, and then in the 1870s wallpaper and fabrics.

A room furnished in Arts and Crafts style, designed by Gimson

Morris designs are still sold today, and his wallpaper designs featuring huge naturalistic flowers were very influential.

Morris and his firm were modestly successful, and in 1882 the Century Guild was formed, producing furniture, fabrics, and metalwork. They took plant-forms as their inspiration, and were into fretwork. In 1884 the Art Workers' Guild was started, and in 1888 a society was instituted to take Arts and Crafts ideas to the masses.

One of the most important firms run on Arts and Crafts lines was Kenton & Co., specializing in hand-made furniture, both heavily inlaid and simple (typical cottage furniture). The primary furniture designers were Ernest Gimson and the Barnsley brothers. The more simple furniture is ageless, but some of their work has a gawky look about it, anticipating the robust and angular furniture of *art nouveau*. The somewhat impractical furniture that came out of the movement was superbly made, and is now much collected. The methods of the Arts and Crafts people convinced up-and-coming designers that this was the way to go. Why should simple things not be beautifully made?

The dilemma lay in the problems of mass producing beautiful things, though Ambrose Heal came nearer than most in coming to grips with them. Heal and his contemporaries preferred plain unpainted wood, waxed not stained, and in doing so laid the ground of the present pre-occupation with stripped pine. Heal's of Tottenham Court Road is a reminder that the Arts and Crafts Movement had its disciples. Another important man was Gordon Russell, who was involved in the fitness for function movement and the postwar world of G-plan.

The lunatic side of the Arts and Crafts Movement had an effect, too. The worst of arty and crafty can be seen in the products of the fringe craft workshops, such as the Omega Workshop, which flourished 1913–19, in which the furniture and other pieces were not only hand-made but badly made and resembled the products of a school handicraft class.

The early work of the Arts and Crafts pioneers such as William Morris are highly rated. Morris, Marshall, Faulkner & Co., produced a lot of stuff, but a piece designed by Morris and made by his workshops should not always be taken on trust. It is easy to get mixed up with Arts and Crafts and *art nouveau*, and attention should be paid to the quality rather than the label the objects are travelling under. The crafts workshops produced a lot of tiles; William de Morgan is the main name to look for in this field.

Arts and Crafts designs are rural rather than urban; cities were bad and villages were good, so it is not surprising that there is a preponderance of rustic themes. The old was better than the new, and so we see the designers harking back to medieval themes (as Morris's friend the painter Rossetti did). That their conception of the middle ages was idealistic rather than accurate did not prevent them re-creating handsome chests with massive locks and chunky cupboards that would have puzzled their ancestors rather than delighted them.

Bottles

The bottle was the first disposable container, and there are two main kinds, those made of glass and those made of pottery, though leather and paper (from 1887 onwards) have been used. Glass is the best because of its versatility, but its one snag was its inability to withstand boiling water though toughened glass has solved that problem.

Colourless glass was made in England as early as the fourteenth century; by 1696 there were eighty-eight glass factories in England, thirty-nine making bottles. In 1746 the government imposed a stiff duty on glass, making it an expensive raw material. This led to a boom in engraved glass; if glass was dear anyway, manufacturers decided to make it into a prestige product.

Blown glass left a rough bit at the bottom (the pontil mark), so to prevent wine bottles falling over the bottom of the bottle was pushed in when the glass was ductile. This 'kick-up' is still found on wine bottles, though the reason for it was lost when bottles were moulded. Wine was one of the first liquids to be put into glass bottles. Wine bottles were originally bulbous and spherical, but this made them difficult to store horizontally (wine is stored horizontally so that the cork is moist, thus stopping air getting into the bottles).

By Victorian times bottles had a modern shape. Early wine bottles were light green in colour (iron oxide in the mix), but Victorian wine merchants made the glass darker – dark green, brown, even black – to prevent the buyer seeing cloudy or sediment-swimming wine. Beer did not get into bottles until the eighteenth century as the glass was more expensive than the product.

Wooden moulds were used to make square bottles for the spirit trade, then for cylindrical bottles but the necks, lips and shoulders of the bottle were hand-formed. With the coming of metal moulds lips with an internal screw thread could be made (screw tops date from 1872). Metal moulds made it possible for bottle manufacturers to advertise the products contained in the bottles by embossing.

Old beer and wine bottles do not cost much; the most desirable wine bottles are the spherical shaped ones or those made for the gentry with their various emblems added as a seal, though Victorian manufacturers copied this to give the product prestige. Being gaseous mineral waters and ginger-beer were kept in

A fine bottle of 1755 (*Horniman Museum*)

stoneware bottles; these are not necessarily old, being in production until quite recent times. Another fallacy is that bottles with marbles in the neck are old; these were made until World War II in India. They were patented by Hiram Codd ('Codd's wallop') in 1875.

More interesting bottles were provided for the medical and cosmetic industries, coming in all shapes, sizes, and colours. Patent medicines often came in impressive bottles with their merits acid-etched into the glass or transmitted on pompous paper labels. Most attention has been focussed on ink bottles, which exist in extraordinary varieties. The lips are often 'sheared' so that the glass cuts into the cork and prevents the ink escaping.

Every collectors' fair is sure to have a stall devoted to bottles, but those with a taste for adventure can find their own in streams, canals, and rivers especially in industrial areas. Tips and rubbish dumps are another source, but no one needs to be told about toxic waste and the dangers lying in wait for the unwary. And be careful of a bottle's contents; prussic acid is prussic acid whether or not it is in a pretty bottle.

Brass and Copper

Brass and copper have the advantage that they fit into the homes of almost everyone. They have the no-nonsense air of being functional, even if no one is going to use a brass kettle for the tea or a Georgian copper pan to cook bacon and eggs in, and they appeal to the kind of person who is not particularly interested in antiques as such. As with furniture, they were made for long, hard use. The colours of brass and copper, from dull yellow to glowing reds, fit in with modern schemes of decoration, particularly those in country cottages and farmhouses.

Certain brass and copper items can be collected for use. Andirons and firedogs can grace the open hearth (andirons are metal bearers which support logs as they burn, firedogs are similar but smaller). When coal replaced wood as the customary fuel andirons and firedogs became obsolete, but now that the wood fire has come back into its own they are with us again. Brass bedsteads have become very popular, but the signs are that their prices are settling; they were introduced in the mid-nineteenth century as more sanitary than wooden bedsteads. Cheaper versions were made of cast-iron with brass trimmings.

Candlesticks come in all shapes and sizes, and in country areas are priced on the high side. In early brass candlesticks there was a large greasepan halfway down the shaft, but in the eighteenth century this was replaced by a pan near the top. There was often a sliding device to remove a candle stump, or raise or lower it. During the nineteenth century candlesticks became extremely ornate, and with the coming of the oil lamp and gas were not so essential in the home though the chamber or bedroom candlestick, with a large pan and handle, kept its place.

The chestnut roaster consists of a hinged box with holes in it on the end of a long handle. They are decorative and have been reproduced in large quantities, as have coal-scuttles, usually made in two shapes, the helmet and the shovel. The genuine ones are heavier and almost always have signs of wear – they were never made to be ornamental. Brass door-knockers were ornamental and useful. The lion's head, widely used on the doors of churches and cathedrals, has proved a firm favourite, and so have those incorporating classical features – rams' heads, dolphins, and the like. Small knockers, allegedly for rooms inside the house, are not usually old.

There are a wide variety of brass and copper jugs and ewers, old and new, solid and sturdy or wafer-thin with cheap stamped designs on them. Once again the prospective buyer should look for thickness of metal and signs of use. Plaques are almost always modern decorative pieces. The grate, brought into being by the use of coal instead of wood, was sometimes of brass, more usually of cast-iron. Fenders were used with wood fires, but mainly date from the age of coal, often matching the metal of the grate. Eighteenth-century fenders were low, often with a base of sheet iron to keep the structure rigid and to hold glowing embers that had fallen from the fire. Victorian fenders were higher and more ornamental, and *art nouveau* contributed to fender design.

Along with grates, fenders and other fire furniture were fire-irons – shovel, poker, and tongs. Steel was favourite, with copper or brass detail or handles; all-brass is usually later and seem to be preferred by collectors not primarily interested in using them.

Brass and copper bugles, horns, and most blowing instruments should be treated with suspicion. They are best-sellers in tourist traps; by their nature they should be uncommon, and this they decidedly are not. Horse-brasses are widely reproduced; the older ones are smoother and if they are turned over there are no rough edges or unsightly pits, the signs of haste and a cheap job nastily done. They did not come into general use until the nineteenth century, so the old ones are not really very old.

Oil-lamps have become very expensive, especially those with ornamental globes. Most of those about are later than 1859 when the paraffin lamp was invented. And, of course, brass oil-lamps are widely reproduced, as are brass trivets and warming-pans. In puzzling out whether a warming-pan is old (and they were made at least from the sixteenth century) the wooden handle is perhaps more profitably examined than the pan itself. Wood ages gently, and forcing the ageing process shows.

No class of antique lends itself more to large-scale reproduction than old copper and, especially, brass. It needs a keen eye to tell whether it is old brass or brass deliberately 'distressed'. Fortunately the makers of reproductions are their own worst enemies. Their joins are too neat, and they are mean with the metal. Everything is machine-made for the machine-age, and their monument should be the ubiquitous brass bell, too small and useless to impress anyone. A quality modern reproduction is a different matter, but if it is honest and well-made why shouldn't it be acceptable? Age is not necessarily a virtue in itself.

Button Hooks

Button hooks have never been, nor ever will be, expensive. Their range is limited, but this might be an advantage. With many small things the variety is inexhaustible, and there is no hope of getting an entirely representative collection together, while with button hooks nearly every kind that has been made can be gathered.

What was a button hook used for? To pull the buttons of gloves and especially boots through the holes. They had to be hard-wearing, strong, with a smooth hook. Buttoned boots appeared about the same time as Queen Victoria ascended the throne, and throughout the rest of the nineteenth century buttons became more numerous particularly when tall boots came into fashion. A button hook was a necessity, not a luxury – that is why there are a lot about, often with silver or silver plate handles, though mother-of-pearl, bone and ivory were widely used. The silver is very thin, and spread over a metal core. The hook part is usually steel, some-times bone or ivory, occasionally brass.

For the bottom end of the market, all-steel hooks were produced, often stamped with an advertising slogan and given away at shoe-shops. The silver handles were usually nicely designed using the same kind of motifs familiar on Victorian cutlery. Hooks are sometimes found with a shoe horn in a set, but nobody can raise much enthusiasm for shoe horns.

Buttoned boots largely died out at the beginning of World War I except among the older generation who continued to wear them until the boots dropped off or were replaced in the fullness of time by new-fangled slip-in shoes.

Buttons

If a collector has pence rather than pounds to spend, a wide open field is the button. It is also an ideal introduction to collecting for children. Naturally there are buttons that do fetch a good deal of money such as the enamel buttons of Limoges, but even silver buttons or buttons set with semi-precious stones are inexpensive.

There are two kinds of buttons, those with a shank of metal or material and those pierced with holes. Each of these types is divided into two classes, buttons that are composite and made of two or more pieces, and those that are simple discs of a single material. Buttons were made for use or show, and an acceptable gift to a nineteenth-century lady was a set of silver or semi-precious stone buttons, often packaged in a velvet-lined case and provided with a split ring attachment so that they could be used as brooches.

The materials used in making buttons are almost endless – brass, iron, ivory, bone, horn, glass, porcelain, pottery, enamel, paper, wood, leather, tortoiseshell, ebony, mother-of-pearl. In 1689 brass buttons were first made in Birmingham, but less utilitarian were the hand-stitched buttons of the eighteenth century where silk, mohair, cotton, and even gold wire were knitted over wooden moulds. Mass production of buttons began in 1745, and in 1807 decorative buttons began to be produced in which two discs of metal were locked together by having their rims turned back on each other. These discs had a filling of cloth or other material, and by making a pattern in the upper disc very attractive buttons were produced.

The demand for buttons in the nineteenth century was immense. The railways, the fire services, the police, and the post office had their own livery and their own custom-made buttons. So did the servants of the rich, and buttons were made bearing the family coat of arms or crest, either genuine or thought up for the occasion. These buttons are so various that they lend themselves to collecting, but for the exotic we must go to the world of fashion. Buttons could be miniature art works, illustrating Biblical and Classical themes or depicting well-known personalities such as the ballet dancer Taglioni. Children's buttons had nursery rhymes on them. Porcelain buttons were supplied as blanks for the purchaser to paint in her own picture.

Transfer printing as used in pottery provided patterns on buttons. A block of buttons was covered with an overall design; these were known as 'calicos' because the design resembled calico cloth. Glass was widely used. 'Kaleidoscopes' are clear glass buttons with a paper design glued between the glass and the metal backing. Better quality glass buttons are miniature paperweights. There was also a wide variety of coloured glass used, as well as synthetics such as celluloid.

In the 1880s men's fashions demanded the greater use of buttons, and *art nouveau* also encouraged new designs, swirly and sinuous. In the 1920s and 1930s new ranges of plastics provided the chance to make vivid buttons and buttons with extravagant shapes, and since then campaign, advertising, and jokey buttons have added to the variety available.

Every bric-à-brac stall in a street market has a tin of buttons to browse through. For a couple of pounds you can build up a big collection; for ten pounds you could fill a cabinet.

Chessmen

Chess historians differ in their opinions on the age of the game, but some time between 3000 BC and AD 500 is acceptable to most. Modelling chessmen into individual forms dates from the twelfth century. The Hindus carved ivory to represent opposing armies, the Arabs used abstract shapes as their religion forbids the representation of people, and the British used jewelled gold and ivory pieces. The rules changed over the centuries, and certain pieces were given increased powers or had their names altered (the alphyn became a bishop).

In Britain chess became such a widespread pastime that laws were passed forbidding the common people to play except on holidays. For lesser mortals, chesspieces were carved in wood, but for the wealthy no material was neglected and no design was too extravagant. A school of ivory-carvers arose in Britain in the eighteenth century just to cater for the great demand for chesspieces in that substance. Amber, agate, glass, and horn were also employed.

The design of British chessmen became plainer after about 1820, and the bodies of the queen and king were abstracted into squat cones. In 1847 the Staunton chessmen made their appearance; these established the standard look of chessmen to the present day. The earliest porcelain chessmen date from about 1750, and Meissen made them from 1758. Wedgwood came on to the scene in 1783, making chessmen in several colours and selling them at five guineas a set. These moulds were used until 1931, turning out blue and white chessmen for the pleasure of chess-players and the occasional puzzlement of chessmen collectors.

Pottery chessmen, also produced by the Wedgwood factory, were slightly cheaper than porcelain but at more than three pounds a set they were far too expensive for the man-in-the-street, who was catered for by simpler mass-produced Staunton chessmen in wood.

The most collected chessmen are, of course, the most exotic. The theme of opposing armies has been treated with immense bravura, but the very expertise of the makers can confuse players who have not only to decide what move to play but what a particular figure represents. So far as players are concerned, many prefer to use Staunton men or the plain abstract turned sets; the chesspieces are instruments, not figurines.

When buying a chess set it is important to examine each piece individually for chips and repairs. In bone and ivory sets, the knight (known to the uninitiated as the horse's head) is usually the most vulnerable. It is also necessary to count the pieces to see that there are, in fact, thirty-two. Single chessmen are, of course, collectable in their own right.

As most early gold and silver chessmen were made for private use they were not always hallmarked, and it is possible to mistake modern simulated gold and silver reproductions for the genuine article. There are shops in London which specialize in expensive reproduction chess sets and before venturing into this field, a novice collector should familiarize himself with such reproductions.

Christmas Cards

In 1841 or 1842 a Mr Shorrock of Leith issued a card of a laughing face with the words 'A Gude New Year to Ye'. In 1843 Sir Henry Cole forgot his Christmas letters, and commissioned an artist to design a special greeting card for him depicting a family grouped round a table drinking. It was the first Christmas card, though temperance advocates did not like it. Christmas was not about booze, they declared.

A thousand of these cards were printed in black-and-white, and were coloured by hand, but Christmas cards did not catch on until 1862 when cheap colour reproduction was possible. Many of the illustrations were imported from Germany, and mounted on card in Britain. By the 1880s vast cash rewards were offered for suitable designs, and Lord Tennyson refused a thousand guineas for a series of short verses.

Booklets or fold-overs began in 1884; some of these cards ran to six pages. Newspapers published reviews of new cards, and people stuck their Christmas card collections in albums; one man had 163,000 cards.

As happens today, many of the illustrations had no relevance to Christmas, and cards with Japanese settings had good sales. Birds, dogs, cats and horses were popular in the 1870s, but mistletoe, holly, and robin redbreasts began to be established as sure-fire winners, with lightly-clad maidens also top-sellers. A flood of cheap cards from Austria and Germany depreciated the quality, and privately printed cards made an appearance together with novelty cards, with matches, keys and other small items attached.

There were also frosted cards, padded cards, expensive silk cards, and lift-outs, where holly and mistletoe lay concealed under a flap. The comic card made its appearance, though it had to wait for the twentieth century to make its full impact. For many, Christmas was still thought to be too serious for funny cards, and traditional cards still captured most of the trade, though the Americans were exporting more adventurous cards as early as 1874.

A high proportion of Victorian Christmas cards strike us as gloomy, with pictures of dead robins and churchyard scenes, but many are superbly printed in several colours. They are rarely as exotic as Valentines where lace was used extremely delicately, but there is an immense variety in subject, range of verses (some of them unintentionally humorous), shape and size.

There is no collecting market as yet for twentieth-century cards, though novelty Christmas cards of the 1920s and 1930s are sure to catch someone's eye before long, as well as the 1915 American cards which were, in fact, six-inch records on which greetings were sung in a rich plummy voice of the kind that is all too familiar from television advertisements.

Clocks

Certain kinds of clocks have never gone out of fashion. There has never been a time when long-case clocks (popularly known as grandfather clocks) were neglected completely. Today the demand exceeds the supply, and enthusiasm may outweigh discretion when the chance comes to buy one. It is wise to remember that a brass dial is better than a painted dial, and that an eight-day clock (runs for eight days without winding) is a much better investment than a thirty-hour clock. Early long-case clocks had square, later ones arched, dials, and this applies to bracket clocks.

This is a misleading name, as nothing about them suggests brackets. They were made to stand on a table, and have carrying handles. They were spring-driven pendulum clocks, and are usually well equipped with a variety of striking mechanisms.

A classic Sheraton clock (*Magazine of Art*)

There is glass in the front and back, and the back-plate of the movement is often intricately engraved. They are very collectable, as are skeleton clocks, in which all the works can be seen under their glass domes. There are modern makers of skeleton clocks, but they are usually as good as early ones, and almost as expensive.

Table clocks to clock men mean spring-driven clocks in gilt metal cases dating from the sixteenth and seventeenth century, and are rare birds indeed, as are lantern clocks and Gothic clocks. They belong in the emporiums of the West End and specialist dealers. Carriage clocks are more common, and most people can recognize these. They are usually small, glass-sided, with a carrying handle and a leather case. Carriage clocks are being manufactured today, so something too new and shiny deserves a second examination.

The cheapest and most prolifically spawned antique clock is the mantel clock, without which no Victorian home was complete. They were made in slate with pillars and architectural pediments, in wood cases with plenty of Gothic-type ornament, or in florid pottery mounts. Marble and slate clocks were once so commonplace that no one wanted them, but dealers in clocks found that they often contained excellent movements. So the cases were smashed, and the movement taken away to fit into something more attractive. The poor quality movements in the nastier wooden and pottery cases have by now all broken down, so there is no temptation there; they had built-in obsolescence before the term was invented.

The presence of a pendulum does not mean that the clock is necessarily of quality. All-spring clocks may make pendulums look quaintly aged. The admirable thing about pendulum clocks is that they can be adjusted to become immaculate timekeepers; an old clock which is slow or fast can be regulated. A clock should preferably be going when purchased, but the absence of a clock key means nothing. Clock keys are of a fairly standard size, and most dealers keep a few in a drawer.

With *art nouveau* clocks, the case is often worth considerably more than the movement, and some charming ones were made in pewter, enamel, and pottery. Even when the clock itself is broken, such cases, especially if 'typical', are well worth buying. Shippers buy, for a modest price, the 1920s and 1930s commercial mantel

An elaborate ormolu clock for the Paris Exhibition of 1867 (*Art Journal*)

clocks with or without 'Westminster chimes'. The angular Art Deco clocks of the same period are more desirable properties, particularly if they incorporate statuary or onyx.

Dolls

The doll market has become especially profitable, particularly in America. In early days dolls were whittled from wood or formed from old rags, with no attempt at realism. In the eighteenth century gesso (plaster) was used over wood for the heads, and the dolls were given glass eyes (usually brown without pupils). They were miniature adults, rather than babies; there was more attention paid to their clothes than to their construction.

From about 1825 dolls were wired for walking and sleeping, and china, wax, and paper mâché began to be used. The wax was poured into moulds, or over a papier mâché base: the latter method resulted in surface cracking. When Victoria became queen in 1837 dolls were given blue eyes, as a compliment to her. In the 1870s fully jointed dolls came in.

In wax dolls human hair was put in, strand by strand, but china heads had to be content with a wig. In the early 1860s the French took over from the English as the premier dollmakers, and glazed china was replaced by a matt china (bisque). The names to conjure with are Jumeau and Bru, amalgamated in 1898.

Until about 1880, dolls remained little ladies, but then became *bébés* or plump little girls, a trend that continued until Cindy and Action Man arrived on the scene.

The Germans could not compete in quality with the French, but their greater abilities in marketing and mass-production enabled them to get the lion's share of the international market. The Americans counter-attacked with the gollywog (about 1890) and the teddy-bear (about 1903).

The craze for dolls has meant that the products of the 1930s and 1940s are snapped up, and that even relics of a nursery fire or the attacks of an enraged infant are lovingly resurrected for the boom. Black dolls are worth more than white dolls. But the nineteenth-century dolls are the pick of the bunch, pop-eyed as they might be and as bald as badgers as their wigs disintegrate.

Ethnographica

There is no easier way to burn one's fingers than with ethnographica. A fairly new collecting category so far as general dealers are concerned, ethnographica is a wide field pertaining to native arts and artefacts, with African masks and Maori weapons at the top end of the market and touristy carved animals at the bottom. Materials vary, with wood predominant. Any ethnographica in metal, especially bronze, is worth more than a cursory glance, and even crude stone carvings may be Eskimo and worth several hundred pounds each.

The kind of ethnographica much in demand, an Eskimo whalebone carving (*Magazine of Art*)

The European collector has to look at ethnographica in a new light, discarding generations of familiarity with Western art, and this, to say the least of it, is difficult. It is hard to differentiate genuine vigour from mere crudity, even harder to decide what is old and what was made yesterday. Old is also relative. Nineteenth century can be old in the field of ethnographica.

Carvings carried out recently were not necessarily done with intent to deceive; many carvers were simply working in the old traditions, only lightly touched by progress, but as the middle men come in so does a touch of cunning. It does not need a strenuous dose of the ageing process to knock a hundred years off a carved figure or mask, merely the will to believe.

The only way to get to know ethnographica is to study it in

A group of 1880s ethnographica – Fiji pottery (*Magazine of Art*)

specialist shops or in museums, and get the feel of it, deciding whether a bit of pattern looks right and what the craftsman was trying to say. A feeling for wood helps. The black wood so many carvings are carried out in is usually a give-away, shouting out modernity. Novices are advised to steer clear of black wood and, indeed, ethnographica unless they get to know it.

Furniture

No one needs to be told that furniture is useful as well as ornamental. Some of the ugliest furniture ever made – the over-stuffed all-embracing armchair of the 1930s – was incomparably comfortable. The oak chairs of the seventeenth century are desperately uncomfortable, though beautiful. Most old well-made furniture is expensive today; but so is well-made new furniture. And new furniture will not appreciate in value, so on the most mundane level old, not necessarily antique, furniture is a good buy.

Most dealers recognize the 'standard' pieces of furniture, though it is astounding what gaps appear in their knowledge when they are put to the test. It is nothing odd for dealers with many years' experience to mistake reproduction Edwardian furniture for their Georgian and Regency originals. By standard pieces we mean cabriole-legged chairs, bureaux, D-end tables, Sutherland tables, loo tables and, the most famous of Victorian articles, the chaise longue. If reasonably priced, none of these will stay long in a dealer's shop, and at auctions there will be no shortage of bidders. If they do stick in a shop, either they are outrageously priced or there is something wrong with them – perhaps a 'marriage' has taken place. A marriage is a made-up piece of furniture, something from this, something from that. Tables are very prone to this.

It is fair game for anything off the beaten track, or furniture which for some reason is not liked – by dealers. When cabriole-legged furniture was going through the roof, the same kind of thing with turned legs could hardly find a market. While very ordinary Victorian furniture was waxing rich, beautifully made Edwardian furniture was going for a song. That has changed now, but Edwardian mahogany is still undervalued, as is the more restrained Victorian furniture. The continental, Australian and American buyers liked their Victoriana ornate; but a lot of

An elaborate Victorian piece of the type much in demand (*Art Journal*)

A classic piece of furniture, a Chippendale double chair (*Magazine of Art*)

Victorian furniture was not, especially that made in the country where craftsmen continued to work without the benefit of technological advances. The furniture produced by the anti-capitalist workshops, and Aesthetic and Arts and Crafts furniture has yet to be taken up systematically, though shrewd shippers are boning up on it, leading to a modest run on bamboo and simulated bamboo furniture of the 1870s and 1880s. But no one has yet latched on to the possibilities of ebonized furniture. Black-painted furniture (which is what ebonized furniture really is) stays in the doldrums, despite its elegance and quality, which is far higher than the 'trade' furniture of the period.

It is perhaps a mistake being overimpressed by the period from which a certain piece of furniture comes. There are trends in furniture, as with all things. After the last war there was a Regency rage, and more recently there was the Victoriana fad. There are craftsmen in all ages (even machine-made furniture has to have a guiding spirit), and it is worthwhile to ask how *well* an article of furniture is made, whether it does what it sets out to do without falling over or irritating the user, and how it looks. A useless piece of furniture is useless whether it was made in the eighteenth century or yesterday. One has to use a certain amount of discretion. No one would discard a Georgian looking-glass because the mirror has lost its silvering, but equally one would not put it in a bathroom and expect to shave by it.

If one is looking for serviceable furniture that fits in with modern needs, that is out of the usual run, and yet is inexpensive it is worthwhile looking at quality between-the-wars furniture. This has not yet been systematically tabulated, and the dealer gets what he can without being influenced by price guides. Things to look for are the quality of the fittings, the wood, and the finish. The 1920s and the 1930s were lavish in the use of exotic woods, such as zebra-wood, birds-eye maple, satinwood, and especially beautifully figured walnut. If the piece is intended to lie against a

The kind of furniture one is unlikely to see outside a museum or a stately home, a Louis XV chest (*Magazine of Art*)

46

A brass bed, so long scorned, then so popular. Bur rarely so elaborate as this one of 1867 (*Art Journal*)

wall, such as a sideboard, do not be put off by a plywood back – even quality furniture was fitted out with plywood (usually five-ply), and it did not carry overtones of cheapness.

Glass

Glass is one of the most versatile and cheapest mediums known to man. There is vast scope for a collector who chooses to concentrate on one of the less known types and not collect old drinking glasses, Cranberry (also known as ruby glass), or Mary Gregory (cameo-like figures against the surface of the glass). By selecting some uncollected kind of glass there is less chance of falling foul of fakes. Techniques have hardly changed over the centuries and there is little secrecy about processes so that a modern forger has a wide field. Some of the best fakes come from Czechoslovakia. This is not surprising as Bohemia was the centre of glassmaking in the nineteenth century.

It is comparatively easy to tell the difference between cut glass and moulded glass. The ornament on cut glass is sharper, and in moulded glass there is usually a narrow ridge running down the glass which betrays its origin. The various types of glass are named according to its ingredients: lead glass contains lead, flint glass powdered flint. Crystal glass is virtually meaningless, as its definition changes with the centuries.

Glass decoration can be carried out during the making of the glass (such as letting bubbles into the ductile glass to produce 'air-twist' stem glasses) or after. Engraving is done by revolving copper wheels, which slices the surface, or by diamond-point, which creates a pattern or a picture. When one says 'after', this may be two hundred years after. A glass may be old, but the design may have been done yesterday – and there is no way of knowing.

The most open field for a collector lies in nineteenth-century coloured glass. There is agate glass (also called slag glass, mosaic glass, and end-of-day glass) which is purply with white or grey veins running through it, popular in vases and bowls. Amberina glass is two-toned with air bubbles, bronze glass is self-descriptive, Burmese glass is greeny-yellow shading to pink, candy stripe glass has bands of alternating plain and colour, cobalt blue glass is so dense it has been mistaken for porcelain, iridescent glass has the sheen of a soap bubble, while milk glass is opaque white, and was often painted on by amateurs. Bristol glass is a general name given to eighteenth and nineteenth century coloured glass. Opaline glass can mean milk glass, or opaque glass in a number of colours.

There is no energetic search for any of these fascinating varieties. Even 'Carnival glass' (a sickly yellow-orange) commands only £2 or £3 a piece, despite it being shipped to America in quantity. And not only is the glass itself interesting. The most amazing objects were made in glass. Some are collected, some are not. There are busts, table centrepieces, door stops, hand coolers (glass eggs, widely reproduced today), paperweights (even more widely reproduced), and such novelties as shoes and slippers, hunting horns, blown glass ships, birds and animals, and walking sticks (sold at fairs and often containing sweets). The quality of such pieces is often very fine, particularly items at the top end of the market such as scent-bottles.

Glass was ideally suited to *art nouveau* tastes, and much of this was derived from plant forms or organic shapes which sometimes gives *art nouveau* an agreeable sloppy look, as though the glass had grown rather than been created by the hand of man.

As we all know, glass is very vulnerable, and sometimes it is hard to spot any imperfections, especially on spiky cut glass. It is extremely difficult to carry out a satisfactory repair job on glass. On the other hand, a few minute chips off something ornate are less obtrusive than would be the case in the same sort of thing in porcelain. The rims of drinking glasses sometimes have minute chips out of them or are 'nibbled', and the best way to detect such faults is to rub a finger round the rim. The sense of touch is far more reliable than the eye. An imperceptible crack can be discovered by 'ringing' the glass – flipping it with a finger-nail so that it rings out.

Nineteenth-century glass is something of a neglected area. One of the reasons is that experts find it difficult to assign various pieces. Nailsea (established in 1788) is one of the big names in novelty glass, but few can hope to determine whether a specific piece came from there or one of the many other manufacturers. Glass does not lend itself to the mystic symbols and initials that make pottery and porcelain so endlessly fascinating to connoisseurs.

Glass Paintings

Glass paintings are a form of print, and are properly called transfer engraving. The first 'glass painting' was produced by John Smith in 1699, and for the first fifty years mainly portraits were made.

The method was to take an engraving, soak it in water, dry it, and lay it, face down, on glass spread with turpentine. The back of the print was then rubbed with a sponge or finger until the paper was all but taken off, leaving just the shadow of the print on the glass. Varnish was next applied, and when this was dry the print, or what was left of it, was painted from the back.

It was a curiously effective way of providing a simulated oil painting, and engravings were made especially to be used as the basis of glass paintings. Sometimes the putting-down of the print was done casually, and little bits of white paper were left on the glass.

The painting was usually done fairly broadly, and the glass picture does not look like the usual coloured print often having the appearance of a primitive. Glass paintings have become very popular, and are often put into fashionable maple frames. An industry has evolved producing modern glass pictures using much the same method. The accent here is both on the quaint and the sporty.

Glass pictures do not suffer from the same ageing processes as prints, such as foxing and general scruffiness, but in many pictures there has been a tendency for the paint to crack or splinter off. Often a successful restoration can be carried out; working from the back, of course.

Gramophone Records

By gramophone records we mean shellac 78 r.p.m. records and not 45 and 33 r.p.m. extra-play and long-play discs, and although many 78 r.p.m. performances have been transferred to long-players this does not matter to the purist. The 78 r.p.m. is the original, and that is what matters. Many performances, however, exist only in 78 r.p.m. form, and the enthusiasts for this or that

An early Columbia gramophone (*Science Museum*)

artist will go to almost any lengths to sort out rare discs.

There are hundreds of thousands of records about. In the 1920s the gramophone was far more popular than the wireless set. Many records have been thrown away, but many people have held on to theirs, hoping to find time to play them. Most people don't, and there comes a time when they get rid of them. Gramophone records are heavy and space-consuming, as well as fragile, and many antique dealers would rather not know about them, leaving them to junk shops and market-stall holders, ignoring the fact that specially choice items command ten or twenty pounds or even more.

Classical records, unless they feature collectable soloists or are old (pre-World War I), are not highly rated. The most sought after soloists are singers, especially operatic singers, though there are some, such as Caruso, who made vast quantities of records and there is a thin line between the collectable Caruso and the run-of-the-mill Caruso.

Pioneer records are always worth getting hold of. They were one-sided, and the title was engraved into the wax. The coming of the paper label is a good guide line. An inordinate number of early records feature military bands. These are not much collected. They were recorded simply because the tone of the military band was more faithfully reproduced than that of an ordinary orchestra.

Among the worthwhile 78 r.p.m. categories are music-hall comedians, early ragtime (which came in a few years before World War I), 1920s and 1930s dance bands, and pre-World War II jazz. But collectors of 78 r.p.m. records cover a wide area. There are Peter Dawson collectors, Harry Lauder fans, and even people who will buy everything Troise and his Mandoliers put on shellac. Prices are flexible – from 20p a record upwards; it is a question of gauging the demand, and even the trade-scorned classical records have their enthusiasts.

Condition plays an important part in the buying and selling of records. They were meant to be played with steel needles, and although this gave a crispness that is astounding even in these days of hi-fi they did wreck havoc on the surface. Sometimes the signs of overwear are difficult to see, but there is usually a change of surface colour where the needle has bitten in. Scratches are worse

WHAT WILL YOU DO

IN THE

LONG, COLD, DARK, SHIVERY EVENINGS,

WHEN YOUR HEALTH AND CONVENIENCE COMPEL YOU TO STAY

INDOORS ?

WHY!!! HAVE A PHONOGRAPH, OF COURSE.

It is the FINEST ENTERTAINER in the WORLD.

There is nothing equal to it in the whole Realm
of Art.

It imitates any and every Musical Instrument,
any and every natural sound, faithfully :

the **HUMAN VOICE**, the **NOISE OF THE
CATARACT**, the **BOOM OF THE GUN**,
the **VOICES OF BIRDS OR ANIMALS.**

From

£2 2s.

THE GREATEST MIMIC.

A Valuable Teacher of Acoustics. Most Interesting to Old or Young. A Pleasure
and Charm to the Suffering, bringing to them the Brightness and Amusements of
the outside World by its faithful reproductions of Operas, New Songs, Speeches, &c

EVERY HOME WILL sooner or later have its **PHONOGRAPH** as a **NECESSITY.**

HAVE YOURS NOW ; you will enjoy it longer.

Brought within the reach of every family by Mr. Edison's last production at **£2 2s.**

Send for our Illustrated Catalogues to

EDISON-BELL CONSOLIDATED PHONOGRAPH CO., LD.,

Or to our Licensees—

39, Charing Cross Road, W.C.

EDISONIA LD., 25 to 22, Banner Street, and City Show-Rooms, 21, Cheapside, E.C., LONDON.

An interesting advertisement for a 1901 phonograph (*The King*) than wear, and can make a favoured record worthless.

Bad storing has resulted in many records becoming 'bowed' (ie turning up at the edges). This does not affect the playing, but makes them vulnerable when restacked. The bowing can be cured by immersing them in near-boiling water and placing them between two sheets of plate glass while pliable, taking care to dry the record after treatment.

Ivories

Although ivory usually comes from elephant tusks, it can come from other mammals, such as the rhinoceros and the walrus. It serves a number of uses, both decorative and functional, and it can be confused with other substances, such as the cheaper bone, and the even cheaper celluloid, not to mention modern plastic. It is easier to discriminate between ivory and bone than between ivory and an ivory imitation. (This can be done by setting light to it – drastic but effective. Ivory does not burn.)

Among the items made of ivory are chessmen, the veneer on good quality piano keys, buttons, jewellery, boxes, tea caddies, fans, needlework accessories, the backs of dressing-table sets, and miniatures of all kinds. Ivory comes in a variety of hues from a glowing white to a faded brown, and it is ideal to carve as it does not split or splinter – thus its worth to miniaturists. It should not be kept in a centrally heated room (ivory warehouses are underground and unheated).

The most celebrated ivory-carvers were those of Dieppe, but their fame has been eclipsed in the sale room by the anonymous French prisoners-of-war who carved ivory and bone ships whilst under detention. Some of these carvings, allegedly by Frenchmen, were done by American prisoners-of-war in England. Less well-known are the English 'Voyez' ivories, box-tops in open work, intricate and delicate landscapes and sea scenes. Some of the same cleverness can be seen in the tracery of ivory fans.

Small ivory items are by no means expensive, and a collector on a small budget would do well to consider them as a suitable field, preferably concentrating on Western examples of the art, for with Oriental ivories we are on dangerous ground. This is especially true of netsukes. Netsukes are toggles, and were brought into being by the fact that in Japan no one had pockets in their garments. Personal items were carried on a cord attached to the belt by a netsuke. Netsukes were made of jet, coral, jade, amber, and porcelain, but those made of ivory particularly attract collectors. From the 1860s, when Western dress began to become popular in Japan, netsukes have been exported, often being palmed off on ignorant Europeans as being the work of known masters. Netsukes were faked a century ago, and they are just as readily faked today.

Jelly Moulds

Jelly moulds belong to a useful category of antiques that can be utilized as well as displayed. They come in three main types – pottery, porcelain, and copper, the latter being the most in demand. Jelly moulds were mentioned in a cookery book of 1753, and were made by most of the best-known manufacturers including Wedgwood. Jelly moulds are either simple single moulds, large or small, or are in two sections, one inside the other. Liquid jelly was poured into the outer case, and the inner case was pushed in after it, resulting in a layer of jelly between the two. When the jelly was set, the outer mould was lifted off, and the jelly was placed on the table leaving the decorated inner case showing through the jelly.

Jellies were sweet or savoury, and depending on the shape of the mould came in obelisks, wedges, castles, and various fruit and animal shapes. Some of them had a hole in the middle, no doubt a repository for other goodies.

Copper jelly moulds usually had a lining of tin to facilitate the turning out of the jelly and to prevent the copper poisoning anybody. They are unquestionably far more handsome than most of the stoneware moulds that turn up, and it is no secret that a group of routine jelly moulds slightly crazed with age is a rather boring lot. Nor that ex-collectors of jelly moulds are more common than collectors. On the other hand, this keeps moulds circulating. No one has yet bothered about twentieth-century glass jelly moulds, though some of them may be authentic Art Deco; if they are, no one cares.

Jewellery

Newcomers to antiques often find items in antique shops apparently irrationally expensive. Except with jewellery, which frequently seems irrationally cheap. There are few medium range antique shops where there are no silver rings in the four or five pounds bracket, or gold rings for about ten. The same items in a jeweller's window can cost five or six times as much. Even the dealers themselves find this puzzling, and sometimes become uncertain about their judgement, and whether they have been taken in by some gold substitute such as pinchbeck (an alloy of copper and zinc invented in the eighteenth century). Usually they have not. Jewellery in antique shops *is* cheap.

Possibly this is because it is traditional to go to a jeweller's on

Typical Victorian rings, elaborate and vulgar (*Art Journal*)

those occasions where a formal piece of jewellery is needed – such as an engagement or a wedding ring. The act of going to a jeweller's is part of the ritual. But jewellery encompasses all manner of things, and in no other sphere are so many different materials used, from steel to jet, from common plastic to platinum.

If jewellery were straight-forward it would be easier for a novice. There is first of all the question of whether one is looking at real gold, real silver, or precious stones. A hallmark helps, and its presence is a guarantee, but foreign silver is not always marked. Silver can be tested, but the ordinary customer is not likely to have the requisite materials with him or her. It is best to rely on a hallmark. But suppose a hallmark has been applied to base metal?

This is simply not on. It is a skilled job to impress a hallmark into a narrow band of silver, and it is not worth the trouble. Hallmarks are transposed from battered pieces of old silver to more desirable pieces, but there has to be real money at stake to make the operation worthwhile, as the law does not take kindly to this sort of fiddling. Although it would not take in an expert, pinchbeck is similar to gold. If in doubt, if there are no hallmarks, do not buy, though – the value of the gold itself being so small – a gold ring will usually be what it seems. As for stones, it is worth remembering that imitation diamonds (paste) can *always* be marked by real diamonds.

Regarding the precious and semi-precious stones such as opals, amethysts, emeralds, or sapphires, there is no substitute for knowledge – looking at the genuine article in museums or in jewellers, and realizing that it takes a lot to make coloured glass look like gem stones, though jet was systematically imitated in black glass (the so-called French jet). Fortunately real jet is much lighter in weight than it looks.

A good clue to the genuineness of a piece of jewellery is the quality of the fittings – the claw of a ring, the clasp of a bracelet or brooch. Costume jewellery, that general name given to a host of entertaining things, can be good or bad. But a Birmingham trinket manufacturer selling a 'diamond bracelet' at a shilling is not going to spend too much time in fitting a decent clasp.

Most people buying jewellery for themselves have use in mind; it is going to be worn. The great advantage of jewellery is that it is ageless; it would be ridiculous for a woman to wear a crinoline, but not a necklace of the period of the crinoline. The materials are ageless as well. There is nothing silly or old-fashioned about coral or amber (materials still undervalued except by shrewd investors – the coral beds are becoming polluted and there is a boom due). Even the spectacular grand pieces of the nineteenth century, florid perhaps, can be worn to advantage by those brave enough to carry it off. And the clever and ingenious jewellery of the 1920s and 1930s, the cunning mixture of plastic and precious stones and metals and the use of colour, can adorn to the best possible effect the modern miss, mrs, or m/s.

Lace and Linen

It is rare to find male dealers interested in lace, but among the ladies it is becoming an increasingly popular sideline to the more

An intricate piece of mid-Victorian lace by Mrs Treadwin of Exeter (*Art Journal*)

traditional antiques, as it is often beautiful and useful. Machine-made lace can never compete with hand-made, which dates back to the sixteenth century and can be made of a number of different kinds of thread, the most important being cotton, silk, and, the most usual, linen.

There are two principal types of lace, bobbin, pillow, or bone, and needlepoint. Bobbin lace is made on a round or oval pillow, held on the knees or put on a frame. The pattern is drawn on parchment, which is stretched on to the pillow; pins are then inserted around the design. A lace thread is looped around each pin, and then wound around a bone or wooden bobbin. A separate bobbin is used for each thread, and as many as two hundred bobbins may be used for one piece of lace. To avoid confusion, the bobbins are decorated differently or weighted with coloured beads. The wealth of variety in bobbin design has made them collectable items.

Needlepoint is a form of needlework, a sort of embroidery in space, and is sculptural rather than delicate (one of the qualities of bobbin lace). Both forms were used as costume accessories, and lace for the sake of lace is seen at its most subtle as personal adornment, though most interest is in domestic lace, a great proportion of which was made by housewives during the long winter evenings, in which time was no object. This applies to most home embroidery and needlework, whether it be the making of patchwork, the needlework pictures known as Berlin woolwork (the patterns, fabrics, and wools were distributed by Berlin firms), or, that most popular of nineteenth-century pursuits, whitework. Whitework is embroidery worked with a white thread on white ground, much used in table linen. One of the most common forms of whitework is broderie anglaise, where small holes are edged with buttonhole stitches to make an attractive pattern.

Lace and linen are timeless, and we can see how old-fashioned designs have been tamely emulated in nylon. Nylon, no doubt liked by washing-machine manufacturers, lacks both the feel and the rustle of linen, though machine-made lace has its supporters. The home workers of the nineteenth century sometimes used machine-made lace as starting points for their own endeavours.

One difference between bobbin lace and needlepoint is that the threads of the former are twisted or plaited, those of needlepoint untwisted. Machine-made lace is stiffer and the pattern is naturally more regular; the threads of machine-made lace will unravel continuously.

Costume lace can be admired for itself, but it is difficult to show off, unless bravely incorporated in a modern dress. In picture frames, as in museums, it is very boring. Old table- and bed-linen should be checked for weak parts which might suddenly break, but it is often surprisingly resilient and tough. Iron mould can be speedily removed by a proprietary solution obtainable from chemists.

Mechanical Antiques

Mechanical antiques can encompass a wide range of diverse objects, but the one thing they have in common is moving parts, worked by clockwork, gravity, hands or feet, water-power, or even air. Mechanical antiques are mainly of the nineteenth century, when 'the power of spring', meaning clockwork, was paramount. It was the age of the tin toy and of the first typewriters, as well as the sewing-machine.

Tin toys have become very collectable, and even those of the

An unlovely mechanical antique – an early vacuum cleaner (*Science Museum*)

1930s are in high demand, a tin Mickey Mouse toy making several hundred pounds. The evolution of the tinplate industry, particularly in Germany, revolutionized the toy industry. The revival of interest in cheap toys has coincided with notalgia for the transport of the nineteenth and earlier part of the present century, and pre-war Dinky cars and aeroplanes, sold for an old sixpence, fetch astounding prices in the sale room, while the demand for 1920s and 1930s Hornby trains and train-sets cannot be assuaged.

Objects such as old typewriters and sewing-machines have yet to become desirable properties, not possessing the charisma of the fine art of the period nor the efficiency of their modern successors. And there are so many of them about. A modest surge in interest brought out hundreds of old typewriters and sewing-machines from attics and store-rooms, and one Remington looks very much like another. Only the more unusual ones attracted much enthusiasm.

Mechanical antiques can logically include Victorian machinery, and industrial archaeologists are well into this, rescuing steam engines and water-powered mill equipment, though, as ever, they often arrive too late on the scene, preceded by the scrap-metal merchant with ready cash.

Mechanical kitchen equipment, such as cog-driven apple-corers, or early washing-machines, suffer from the disadvantage that they are difficult to set off to advantage. The response of a visitor is often 'So what?'. They are not so picturesque as wooden bowls or the various treen kitchenware (objects made of wood) that can conveniently find a place in the drawing-room. They may be historically significant, and anything out of the ordinary may find a home in a museum, but few can get enthusiastic about them.

Another thing that puts potential collectors off mechanical antiques is that they tend to be heavy and space-consuming. This is important now that people generally live in smaller houses. It therefore needs an interest in mechanical things to thoroughly enjoy mechanical antiques; they are very attractive to those who relish well-made machinery, and also to those who would like to build up a collection of unusual items for a small amount.

One of the axioms of the antique trade is 'Don't buy trouble', and this may be recommended to all collectors, not only to

A CLOCK THAT MAKES TEA!

Calls the sleeper at a given hour, automati cally lights spirit lamp, boils a pint of water for tea, shaving, and other purposes, pours it into a pot, extinguishes lamp, and finally rings second bell to signify all is ready. Invaluable to Ladies, Nurses, Professional and Business Men. It is strong, simple, and in no sense a toy. Prices 25s. to 70s. Postage in United Kingdom 1s. extra. With Foreign orders sufficient postage to cover 11 lb. Weight should be sent.

Please send for Illustrated Booklet, post free from

AUTOMATIC WATER BOILER CO.,
26a, Corporation St., Birmingham,
LONDON OFFICE AND SHOWROOM—

31, George Street, Hanover Square.

A primitive teasmade, an antique of a kind (*Science Museum*) collectors of mechanical antiques. Although splendidly made, such objects as sewing-machines and typewriters have their vulnerable bits – not the cogs and the moving parts, but the basic frame and those parts not of steel. Cast iron is not only easily fractured but becomes pitted by age, and this unsightly surface is difficult to smooth out.

If the idea is to use old typewriters and sewing-machines, remember that typewriters were fitted with a kind of ribbon not easily obtainable today (the Remington used a ribbon of more than an inch in width), and ancient sewing-machines had accessories, the purpose of which is forgotten. The typewriters that used an ink pad instead of a ribbon are unutterably messy. If a typewriter is bought to use it is wise to look closely at the type faces, to see how worn they are. Type faces are replaceable, but the question is whether a modern type face can be found in the style of the original.

Paintings

It is the wish of almost everyone to find a Turner in the attic, and certainly there is more money to be made in the field of fine art than in any other. There are fortunes to be made in pictures; and there are fortunes to be lost. The picture game is very much a lottery, and the names of the artists are swapped like so many counters. But the name signed on a picture should not mean very much, for in no other sphere is fraud and forgery practised so much, and harmless competent paintings are saddled with prestigious names, which, strange to say, are authenticated by so-called experts.

If good paintings were thin on the ground a false signature would show up like a good deed in a naughty world. But there are thousands upon thousands of excellent paintings going the rounds, largely painted in the nineteenth century by amateurs. Amateur in this respect does not mean incompetent; these part-time painters were often ladies and gentlemen of leisure with considerable talent who painted in the traditional styles and spent hours at the galleries copying pictures to improve their technique. Sometimes they did not sign their paintings, sometimes they did; most of them did not get into any works of reference save when they submitted their

The kind of superbly painted picture (by Atkinson Grimshaw) at last getting its just deserts (*Sotheby & Co*)

work to the Royal Academy exhibition and it was accepted.

These paintings, with their original signatures or those more recently added, are in circulation, some of them a pound or two. The prices fluctuate unindexed to quality; often they are set because they are either water-colours or oil paintings. Oil paintings, for some weird reason, are supposed to be worth more than water-colours, though a poor technique is exposed more easily in oils, a poor technique often disguised by trickery (using a sponge to get a leaf effect on trees, for instance, a favourite dodge of the cheap professional painter).

If there is any sphere more wide open to a collector with commonsense and a shrewd eye it is difficult to imagine. A well-painted picture is a good investment if bought cheaply; it may not be a masterpiece, but if it is competent, if it hangs together, if the colour is pleasing, if it is 'like' then, as with all antiques, quality will pay dividends. Experience will enable a collector to differentiate between the slick and the honest.

The best places to buy pictures are in medium range antique shops, where pictures are usually sold at a modest profit simply because they take up valuable wall space and are largely under-

Splendidly executed paintings such as this oil by Schofield can still be found at rational prices (*Sotheby & Co*)

Rather ordinary pictures, such as this one by Louis Wain, command extravagant prices because the artist happens to be trendy (*Sotheby & Co*)

rated, and in auction. The shippers who dominate auction rooms usually fight shy of pictures. Pictures in junk shops are almost always appalling. There are thousands of good paintings; there are tens of thousands of bad ones.

Do not be put off by what is apparently a nineteenth-century picture in a modern frame, particularly if it is a water-colour. Water-colours and drawings are often found in folders, and it is very difficult to sell an unframed water-colour.

Newcomers often buy oleographs under the impression that they are oil-paintings; oleographs are varnished prints, and almost everyone who dabbles in fine art has been taken in at least once. If examined closely, oleographs betray their identity, but if there is still doubt it is wise to look at the back; there is no mistaking picture canvas.

Papier Mâché

Most people have recollections of a sort of paper pudding being made at school or in the kitchen at home – newspaper soaked in water, and then manipulated into sodden shapes which, in the fullness of time, hardened. This was papier mâché, though the real thing was far more presentable.

There were two ways of making commercial papier mâché. One method involved compressing sheets of sized paper into panels, the other paper pulp strengthened with other materials including leaves and other vegetable products. In 1847 a Birmingham firm took out a patent for using steam to make a papier mâché panel pliable, and capable of being moulded into any form, be it sensible – such as a tray – or ludicrous. Papier mâché became a general service plastic, considered suitable for making boxes or pianos.

Papier mâché had long been used, suitably lacquered, in eastern countries for bowls, plates, and small boxes. But that was nothing like the papier mâché from the British factories, which was colourful, adventurous, and thoroughly useful. The articles were lacquered black, and designs were hand-painted on them. The artists, especially the flower painters, were a well-paid élite. Mother-of-pearl was introduced, and this worked particularly well in 'Gothic' scenes where a moonlight effect was wanted.

The objects made in this new versatile material were not cheap; they were directed at the upper end of the market, and only later when papier mâché was mass-produced did it become gaudy and humdrum, with transfers used instead of hand-painting.

Papier mâché was used for trays, writing sets, tripod tables, chairs, fans, boxes, and plaques. The furniture was often strengthened with wood. Papier mâché has proved long-lasting, and the quality of the decorative work is often high. It is Victoriana at its best, and even when Victorian furniture and objets d'art were under a cloud discriminating collectors have kept papier mâché modestly fashionable. It is not therefore likely that nice pieces will be found for nothing, but damaged items can be renovated easily and at little cost. The black lacquering (or japanning) can be re-applied if and when it has been damaged, and the decoration touched up with modern oil paint.

If there is doubt about whether an object is papier mâché or wood, weighing it in the hand will dispel it; wood is much heavier. It also has a grain, which papier mâché never has. A greater danger is being confused by modern pieces in plastic. Vaguely Victorian tripod wine tables are being produced in Italy which have the look of period papier mâché and the weight.

There is much Oriental papier mâché about, especially in the form of trays and boxes, and the decoration is invariably 'typical'. Not much of it is of any consequence, and it is usually available at low prices – far lower than similar items in other materials.

Unlike papier mâché trays or chairs, desk accessories remain within the reach of collectors on a modest budget (*Sotheby & Co*)

Pastry Moulds

Some clues about the style of eating in the good old days are furnished by the kind of kitchen equipment that has come down to us. There was a lot of ceremony as well as eating and drinking, and presentation played a big part. Early in the seventeenth century, the Clerk of the Kitchen who had been responsible for gargantuan Tudor feasts tended to be replaced by a French chef, who brought delicacy into the dining-room. But even the huge game pies of the Elizabethans were decorated; the decoration was produced by pressure from wooden moulds and stamps.

The pastry mould is a blanket term given to utensils that stamped and moulded not only pastry, but cakes, gingerbread figures, and marzipans, biscuits, and small discs of caraway seed powder. The tradition of using pictorial moulds is continued with mass-produced biscuits.

All kinds of designs were used — letters of the alphabet for nursery gingerbreads, heraldic devices and coats of arms, portraits of royalty, animals, carts, sporting scenes in astonishing detail, while fashionable hostesses had moulds made with the likenesses of their coming guests. The favourite wood was pearwood, as it was particularly suitable for carving, but boxwood, beech, apple, cherry, and walnut were also widely used. Most moulds were oblong, but square and round shapes were made, and for marriage feasts heart-shaped moulds were used. Moulds were incised into the wood, or cut above the wood and, considering the high quality of the carving, it is not surprising that the craftsman added his name to his work.

A curious feature of pastry moulds is their thickness, rarely less than $\frac{3}{4}$in and usually an inch or so; this was to insure a good solid impression. They are delightful things to hang on a kitchen wall, and although many of them are rather wormy this adds to the quaintness. There can be confusion between pastry moulds and moulds made for other decorative purposes, such as shaping the plaster used in room decoration. Very occasionally moulds turn up in the shape of a two handled roller — a rolling-pin with a design on it.

Where people had their own chefs and cooks the use of fancy moulds was continued long after mass production brought cakes and biscuits to all, and with the revival of interest in home baking it might be that pastry moulds in good condition might well serve their original purpose of making a meal attractive to the eye as well as to the palate.

Photographs

In 1824, Louis Daguerre produced photographic plates, later known as daguerreotypes. In 1839 Fox Talbot produced the first negative. The daguerreotype is a one-off, and no more copies can be made as the image is on a silvered copper plate; any number of copies could be made from a calotype original. Until 1889, when the celluloid roll film was invented in America, all cameras were plate cameras.

The value of old photographs depends on three factors – when they were taken, the intrinsic interest of the subject, and who took them. Very early photographs are historical objects, and extremely valuable, and so are photographs taken by eminent photographers such as David Octavius Hill, Julia Cameron, and Lewis Carroll. Regarding subjects, the most collectable photographs are those of town or city scenes, especially when they reveal the life of the

Although plain and unassuming, cameras such as this are now much in demand (*Science Museum*)

times. Slum pictures are more valued than photographs of high life and high places.

Daguerreotypes are fragile, easily scratched, and were kept in a frame, usually of leather, with a cover. Calotypes are larger, and are more interesting, as the photographers continually experimented with effects, using tubes to soften the focus and even deliberately employing defective lenses in the camera to obtain unorthodox effects. Most Victorian plate photographs are sepia, and because they were printed on thin paper they have to be handled carefully. Many were stuck in albums and have become badly wrinkled over the years, not to mention being damaged by glue soaking through.

Colouring photographs by hand was carried out from the 1840s, and deliberate attempts were made to make photographs look like paintings. There may not have been any intent to profit by this, but certainly the practice of printing photographs on watercolour paper caused confusion. A hand-coloured photograph rarely carries any extra value.

It is easy to get over-excited by old photographs, especially when they are found in a handsome album, often heavily

The type of old photograph now highly collectable (*Victoria & Albert Museum*)

70

decorated and sumptuously bound, sometimes containing a musical-box movement in the back cover. These albums were made for the carte-de-visite trade; the carte-de-visite was the Victorian studio photograph, and there are, literally, millions of them about. Unless the carte-de-visite is of some well-known person it is of no value except as a curio; hundreds of different photographs were taken of Queen Victoria, and sold in the shops, and these are of no consequence. Neither are photographs of paintings and statuary. A full album sells at between £8 and £15; the album is more desirable than the customary contents.

Stereoscopic photographs are of interest. The stereoscope was introduced in the Great Exhibition of 1851, and continued to hold sway for more than fifty years, either hand-held or in a cabinet. Stereoscopic photographs are in pairs, and when looked at through a stereoscope viewer they appear three-dimensional. There are a lot of them about, mainly views and genre scenes, though there are also pornographic and saucy stereoscopic photographs; these are much collected. English views are considered preferable to continental and colonial scenes.

Most photographs by the major portraitists are documented, and a photograph alleged to have come from the camera of, say, Lewis Carroll should be regarded with suspicion. To the non-expert, one photograph is very much like another.

Not only old photographs are valuable; the experimental 'photograms' of Surrealist photographers such as Man Ray are in great demand, as are original fashion photographs of the 1930s and 1940s and between-the-wars documentary photographs (especially when they have American subjects). Once again, 'originals' must be subject to close scrutiny, not necessarily the photographs themselves but their provenance (ie where they came from).

Picture Postcards

Picture postcards belong to a class of ephemera that deserve to have a section of their own. They have their own magazines, their specialist dealers, and they are enjoying a boom, with some cards valued at more than £15 each, cards that in the 1960s would be hard put to it to make much more than £1 apiece. Picture postcards are in a category which encourages the browser, like stamps and second-hand books.

The first postcard dates from 1869, and Great Britain followed suit in 1870. These were Post Office cards, and not until 1894 did the GPO allow privately printed cards to be sent through the post. Between 1895 and 1900 a squarish card, known as a court card, was used, and two firms, one in Edinburgh and one in Leicester, began printing view cards of their cities. The Post Office insisted that the address should be spread over the entire side of a card, and the message had to be fitted in on the illustrated side. Only in 1902 did the GPO allow postcard makers to split the reverse of the card into two halves, one for correspondence and one for the address.

Postcards were immensely popular, and clubs and magazines grew up concerned with their collection. In an effort to be different novelty and trick postcards were produced — cards that squeaked, cards with revolving centres that were moved by the finger to disclose different views, while every kind of material — silk, leather, aluminium, even peat moss — was used. Postcards served a wide variety of purposes, not merely that of telling the recipient where the sender was. There were advertising postcards, postcards illustrating some current theme, sentimental postcards,

A run-of-the-mill postcard, but collected. Why? Because it shows shop fronts (a desirable subject) in some detail

and, of course, comic postcards. The funny postcard was an integral part of the seaside holiday.

The picture postcard firms employed photographers who would take photos of subjects that other camera-users did not think worth bothering about; they made documentaries whereas others produced 'artistic' photographs. The manufacturers soon found out the best-selling subjects – rough seas, entertainments, transport, actresses, disasters and animals. Louis Wain has become perhaps the best-known of postcard artists through his addiction to cats, though the prices obtained for his work are topped by those obtained for the work of the *art nouveau* designer Mucha, who was not too proud to do postcards as well as posters and general decorative work.

Postcards should be in good condition, unscuffed, with the corners unbent (a fate of many postcards when put into albums); they should have their stamps intact if possible. There are many reputable postcard-dealers; their buying price is usually two-thirds of the selling price. The golden age of the postcard was between 1902 and 1914, and there is less enthusiasm for between-the-wars postcards. Favoured subjects among collectors are trams, omnibuses, railways and railway stations, post offices, aircraft and particularly airships, shop frontages, military subjects, crashes, and exhibitions. Close-ups are better than middle-distance views. Hand-coloured postcards are not much liked, nor are continental views unless they contain some kind of interesting transport. Pictures of churches and cathedrals are actively disliked.

The stamps on the backs of Edwardian postcards are of little value, unless they are unusual foreign or colonial ones.

Pipes

The clay pipe was first seen in England by foreign observers in 1598, an early throwaway product provided free by inns and coffee-houses. The clay pipe came in all sizes, often with a maker's mark impressed; the most famous was the long churchwarden. Cases were made for clay pipes, usually of wood or leather, not because of the value of the pipe but because a traveller preferred an unbroken pipe. Every tip has its quota of bits of pipe.

Clay was a mundane material; porcelain was tried but it burned

A German pipe more for show than for use (*Magazine of Art*)

the smoker's hand and cracked readily. Pottery pipes were more for decoration than use, and so were the glass pipes made in Bristol. Meerschaum was better, unimpressive in its native state but glossy when boiled in milk and kneaded with wax and linseed oil. It was easily carved, but expensive, and imitation meerschaum – lighter yet less porous – was used. Amber and horn were used for pipe mouthpieces, but amber was brittle and was later replaced by ebonite or vulcanite (rubber hardened by heat treatment).

Wood was widely used, preferably cherrywood and rosewood. Quality pipes had their bowls lined with silver. British pipes were inclined to be simpler than those made on the continent, especially in Germany or Austria. Briar ousted other woods from the middle of the nineteenth century; briar is the root of the white heather. Between the wars 25 million briar pipes were exported from Saint-Claude in France, the centre of the industry, to Britain.

Briar lent itself to intricate carving, and a popular novelty was the pipe in the form of a standing figure, whether it was a naked lady or Mr Gladstone. Smoking ages a briar pipe, and it is difficult to tell a fairly modern product from a nineteenth-century pipe, though no one has yet bothered to fake briars, unlike meerschaum pipes. Waste meerschaum was ground into powder and with the help of glue and a mould was re-created into minor antiques, with dates and all.

No one can claim that the collecting of pipes will ever be carried out with any assiduity, but within limits there is a good deal of variety, from the humble clay to the hookah, that over-decorated horror familiar from films of the exotic east. The carved meerschaum is the classic, almost the only one.

Pottery and Porcelain

More has been written about pottery and porcelain than any other antique category. A newcomer to collecting can find it all unnerving, though it is comforting to know that many dealers are in the same boat, picking up casual knowledge as they go along, knowing that Royal Doulton and Royal Worcester are somewhat above the average and that *famille rose* always sells. This may seem somewhat flippant, for most dealers tend to adopt a tone of reverence when speaking of any kind of china that does not come out of the nearest chain store and it is time that someone knocked the mystique on top of the head.

Names and marks on the bottom of china are all very well, but some of the most valuable china has no marks at all. On the other

A 'creamer' made by the Liverpool factory, a collected item and a collected firm (*Magazine of Art*)

hand, some of the most commonplace has all kinds of mystic emblems, including a Victorian patent mark. This is a lozenge-shaped device with divisions. The most collected china is the most faked, and anyone deciding to specialize in, say, Chelsea should take a long hard look at everything bought – and that after an apprenticeship in museums getting to know the genuine article.

Pottery is not necessarily the poor relation of china: it is usually thicker and coarser than china, but not always so. Old Staffordshire is pottery, but that does not stop it being often worth more than the most exquisite china. English china and pottery is a world in itself, but a diligent enthusiast can get to know about it. There is a lot of it about, in antique shops, in stately homes, and in museums. Continental china and pottery is a different matter, and Oriental products are often inscrutable. They have plenty of marks on them, but one Chinese and Japanese set of picturegrams is very much like another.

The best approach to porcelain and pottery is to disregard the marks and names, and go by feel and instinct, at least in the first instance. If it does not appeal, do not buy, even if it is cheap. At present there is a vogue for awful Victorian pairs of vases, at between £8 and £15 a pair. They have always been awful and always will be. No one can really like them, but someone is buying them. Similarly there is a fashion for a certain kind of Oriental ware known as Imari and Satsuma. At best Satsuma vases make good table-lamps, at worst they are loud and vulgar.

Figurines vary from the marvellous to the atrocious, and in this field it is often difficult to separate the art of the craftsman working at a one-off and that of the clever manufacturer turning out thousands of identical models for the tourist trade. If they were not so glaringly new, some of the porcelain figures in gift shops retailing at two or three pounds each would find a ready place in chic antique shops.

The best way to start a pottery and porcelain collection is to buy chipped items for 20p or 30p each and keep them around for a while. If possible hang plates on walls (wire plate-hangers are cheap and efficient). Do not worry about crazing on old pottery; it is a sign of age, and if not too bad does not detract from the value of the piece. And look for craftsmanship – the quality of any hand-painting, the definition of any transfers on blue-and-white, and unusual shapes that show the skill of the potter.

Pottery and porcelain repairing has become a major do-it-yourself pastime, and some of the repairs carried out are very good. The repairers use modern products including fibreglass, and acrylic paints have proved very versatile as colouring agents. A repaired item is still a repaired item, irrespective of how well the job is carried out. With the advent of epoxy resin, broken pieces can be glued together. This is a mixed blessing, as a poor repair cannot be remedied by melting the glue and starting again.

Among under-rated ceramics (the term covering pottery and

A rich exotic Worcester porcelain vase, once disregarded. The kind still to be found, if not quite so impressive (*Magazine of Art*)

porcelain) are dinner services, tea services, and nineteenth-century teapots (often less than half the price of their present-day equivalents). Bisque figurines are beginning to be collected; bisque is unglazed porcelain, slightly sandy in texture. Newly married couples equipping their first home might be well advised to look round antique shops for large useful dinner services before venturing into a shop selling modern ware. Similarly very useful coffee pots can be picked up for a few pounds.

Art pottery can seem to disobey all the laws of the game. It often appears clumsy, with blotches of colour apparently aimlessly placed, but if it comes from one of the collected craft potteries this may not seem to matter, and although potteries such as Moorcroft and Ruskin produced some gripping stuff some of their wares make one scratch one's head. One must be very careful of mass-produced art pottery; in the 1920s and 1930s there was a good deal of adventure among commercial firms, and excellent designers were recruited. We therefore find very striking things coming from Royal Doulton and other ultra-respectable firms. General-purpose pottery and porcelain from the Art Deco period is very much under-rated.

Prints

Prints are often thought of as the poor relations of paintings even though the etchings of Rembrandt and Dürer obtain astronomical sums in the sale room. The term print covers a wide variety of different techniques. The etching is the most aristocratic; the effect is achieved by covering a metal plate with a waxy material and drawing a design in the wax. The plate is placed in acid which eats away the exposed portion. This is done repeatedly, 'biting-in' more design, and 'stopping-out' when necessary. This produces gradations of tone. An etching can be completely altered in the making, and among such masters as Rembrandt the various stages are of significance, from the 'first state' to later states. Etching, because of the subtle qualities possible, is still widely practised. A woodcut is carved out of a block of planed and polished wood. The raised parts will print the design, the scooped out parts being left blank. A wood engraving is the same except that an engraving tool is used instead of a knife. Woodcuts are bold, using big areas of colour or tone, wood engravings are more detailed.

Line engraving is the opposite. The design is cut into a metal plate, the plate covered with ink so that it lies in the cuts, and then the plate is wiped clean. Texture is obtained by closer lines, dots, and cross-hatching. A design in dots is a stipple engraving. As the engraver's burin bites it leaves 'burrs'; these unwanted bits are wiped away, except in a drypoint where they are left to give extra texture. In a mezzotint a 'rocker' is used, an instrument with teeth-like serrations, which roughens up the plate. A scraper is then used on the textured plate. This method gives different tones, rather than lines.

The aquatint is a combination of mezzotint and etching, with the work carried out on a resin surface which dries with a pitting effect. An aquatint can be mistaken for a water-colour, and is perhaps the most subtle of all the printing methods. Certainly the lithograph is the most versatile, and its colour form,

An etching by Sickert, an artist at present out of favour among critics and therefore bound to be good (*Victoria & Albert Museum*)

chromolithography, dominated colour printing from 1837 until the advent of photographic methods fifty years later. The design was made directly on to a specially prepared kind of stone, and a print was taken from the stone. Chromolithography employed a different stone for every colour. It was ideal for large subjects, such as posters. The modern development, off-set litho, has dominated photographic methods of producing prints.

There is no mistaking the slightly chalky look of a lithograph, but there can be confusion about the oil-paint printing processes of George Baxter and his followers. Baxter, whose process dates from 1835, used a succession of wooden blocks, often as many as twenty; he allowed the blocks to overlap, giving fine gradations of tone and colour. In 1848 Baxter was advised to sell licences to other printers, so that they could use his process. He did so, and Le Blond and Kronheim prints are as collectable as those of Baxter. Kronheim used zinc and copper blocks, instead of wood.

There is great scope for print collectors. The categories are without number. Hunting prints have always been popular, but there is still an opening in military and naval prints, though the very big ones fetch high prices. One can still come across Turner prints at a modest cost; sheet music covers, fashion plates, prints of birds and flowers, and railway prints are still available to the impecunious collector – if he eschews the 'classics', Audubon and Gould for birds, the French fashion magazines for their Jules David lithographs. But beware. Many fine prints have been recently reproduced, and a cautious buyer will look for signs of the ageing process. The more unpretentious prints are more likely to be originals – original in the sense of being of their period.

More important than deciding whether a print is a modern photographically produced reproduction (not too difficult) is discerning whether or not a print is a water-colour. There are few dealers who have not been flummoxed. Normally a close examination with a magnifying glass will show the characteristics of the print; and many colour prints will show the plate mark (the ridge round the picture where the plate has pressed the paper). But there are borderline cases. By far the best method is to take the print from its frame, and, taking a small artist's brush dipped in water, try to brush off a little colour. Printing ink does not come off; water-colour does. Every picture has an unimportant area, and a bit of shadow is a good place to try.

This is a good method, but not infallible, for the water-colour may have been varnished. A persistent puzzler might well remove a tiny section of varnish with a solvent. Naturally this can only be done at home; even the most benevolent dealer will draw the line at such operations being carried out in his shop. In the last resort, as with everything, the buyer has to use his or her own judgement.

Rugs and Carpets

To a newcomer, it might seem that the value of a carpet or a rug – especially a rug – is governed by its tattiness and general threadbare quality. Fortunately this is not so. Of more importance than having the appearance of being walked over by a million clogged feet is the number of knots per square inch; these can range from ten to four or five hundred.

Dealers in rugs and carpets are an elect; the art of buying and selling floor coverings of every kind (with the exception of linoleum) is decidedly esoteric, and everything seems to conspire to deter the amateur, or, for that matter, the general dealer. Even the names mystify – what is one to make of Salor, Tekke, Saryq, and Pinde, in the region of Merv? One may well ask where Merv is. Actually these places produce rugs with lozenge motifs on quiet red grounds, and they come under the wider heading of Turkoman rugs, sometimes called Bokhara rugs (they should not be, say purists).

Turkish rugs are different from Turkoman rugs, and there is a healthy export trade in factory-manufactured rugs for the snob market. There are likewise a large number of unpronounceable names for the quality Turkish carpets produced by home looms. Ghiordes rugs are recognized by their refined designs, Kula rugs by their rugged designs, narrow borders, and blues and reds, Melas and Megri rugs by flower patterns, and Ladik, Konya, and Kir Shahr rugs by their arches.

After this, it is a relief to turn to English carpets, to Wilton, Axminster, and the rest of them, and only slightly confusing to find out that these names have nothing to do with towns of origin but are concerned with the type of weave. One does not count knots with English carpets as they are largely machine-made throughout.

After the thin look of Middle Eastern rugs, Chinese carpets are lush and seem to be worth the money they command. A characteristic of Chinese carpets is that the pile is cut round the design to give a relief effect. A general byword for the run of the mill or the cheap and nasty is the Belgian carpet. The Belgian carpet might be termed the 'boarding-house carpet', dull in colour, undistinguished in design, and instantly forgettable.

Because of the overall lack of expertise good carpets and rugs can be picked up at a no greater price than one would pay for a modern equivalent. For less than thirty pounds, a buyer can get something very nice indeed, though a fine Tabriz carpet from Persia should be regarded with suspicion if too cheap (though it might only mean that it is a nineteenth-century commercial carpet for the European market – but well made for all that).

If one is spending more than a hundred pounds on a carpet the wisest and probably the cheapest course is to go to a dealer in carpets and rugs. A specialist dealer depends for his livelihood on giving value for money. A speculation in an auction room for a promising piece of dusty rug may be rash; rugs and carpets can mislead even the shrewdest.

Samplers

The sampler was originally what its name implies – a sample. Its purpose was to lay down stitches and patterns as a primer for needleworkers. By the eighteenth century the sampler had changed its meaning; it was now an exercise in stitching, a chance for a young girl to show off. Long narrow strips of linen gave way to squares and rectangles, eminently suitable for framing.

It was also an instrument of education, with alphabets and numbers incorporated into the all-over design, along with the girl's name and often her age. The date was also put in, very useful to latter-day collectors. Of course, samplers vary in quality, and sometimes a specimen is inclined to be over-rated because of the tender years of the artist – eight, nine, or ten being common.

Many of the samplers are reminiscent of naive paintings or the native work of the Red Indians. Many of the motifs were traditional, with birds, animals and flowers predominating, though more adventurous girls were egged on to do buildings and ships. Where the teachers were religious, Biblical quotes and Bible stories were considered suitable subjects for the busy needle.

Darning samplers, showing a girl's skill in that direction, are less interesting. As the nineteenth century progressed coarser backgrounds were used and silk was replaced by wool, often from Berlin, the makers of which also provided patterns. With less effort girls could produce bolder and more professional-looking pieces, but they were not samplers any longer. There was no longer a diversity of stitch, only one, the cross stitch which became known as the sampler stitch.

Samplers are worth looking for because many dealers do not reckon them at all, and rate them with old linen and flyblown prints as something to get rid of with the minimum of trouble. Good early examples are therefore sold for a pound or two, examples that might cost thirty pounds or more in another shop.

Samplers are fragile, and if they are framed, care should be taken when handling them if they are removed from the frame. If washed, the colours are sure to run. Occasionally it will be observed that dates and ages have been unpicked. There is nothing sinister about this – it merely means that the sampler-maker is disguising her age, anxious to retain evidence of her childish skills but reluctant to admit that she was eleven in 1831.

Scientific Instruments

The scientific instrument-makers, sometimes called the mathematical practitioners, were the élite of the craftsmen until the middle of the nineteenth century, when mass-production began to hold sway. The skills of the instrument-makers were equalled only by gunsmiths and clock and watch makers, and it is difficult to realize that by 1800 instrument-makers were working to a millionth of an inch, precision indeed.

Their products reflect this perfection, and it is not surprising that scientific instruments such as microscopes and telescopes of pre-Victorian vintage are much collected, as are the multitude of nautical instruments such as the sextant. Scientific instruments are distinct from mechanical antiques in that they inform rather than do things. They were created – with the exception of nautical in-struments and those concerned with land measuring such as the theodolite – for men who merely wanted to find out things. These men, fortunately for posterity, were the rich and the influential, the amateur scientists such as King George III and the dilettantes who did not see why they should while away their time in aimless pursuits. The quality of these seventeenth- and eighteenth-century instruments indicate that no expense was spared to create the best

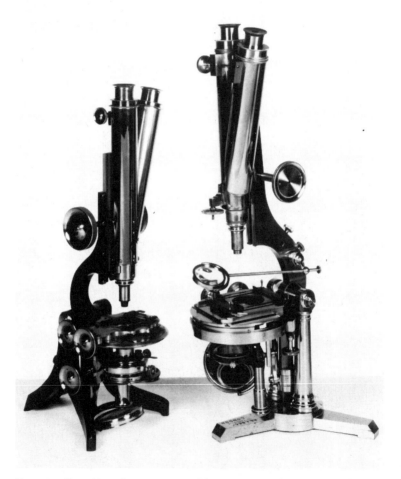

Two magnificent binocular microscopes of the 1860–80 period. Yet the one on the left made only £68 and the other £140 (*Phillips*)

tools for the job, whether it was looking at micro-organisms or searching for new stars.

Sometimes the Victorians did make more efficient instruments. In the earlier ones glass technology was limited and good lenses were hard to come by. But sometimes the old instruments were so good that progress could not improve on them, and the chronometer and the naval sextant hardly altered for half a century or more.

The key metal of the instrument-makers was brass, though other metals, such as steel, were used. Modern scientific instruments make more use of non-reflecting metals, and they are generally more compact, especially when the instrument needs to be portable — such as a surveyor's theodolite.

Even though scientific instruments are collected, they are still not expensive, and a fine Victorian binocular microscope will cost no more than its modern counterpart, and have as good a lens system. Early scientific instruments, those dating from the primitive days of navigation, are prohibitively expensive — most early instruments were to do with the sea. It was not vital to see planets but it was to get from point A to point B as quickly as possible.

Barometers are not strictly scientific instruments. The instrument-makers rather frowned on the makers of barometers and thermometers. Barometers fulfil both useful and decorative functions, but collectors should steer clear of the aneroid barometer, worked by a spring, which is circular and usually in an oak case. Thousands were produced for the Victorian middle classes, and they tend to be unsatisfactory, both as investments and as indicators of future weather.

Some people collect surgical instruments, but this must be a minority interest despite the variety of creepy-looking things available. Drawing instruments are less popular. Despite their names, these two categories are hardly scientific, for they do things rather than inform.

Everyone recognizes a telescope or a microscope, and most people have seen a theodolite in use by council surveyors (it is like a small telescope on a stand). The chronometer, despite its grand name, resembles most of all a large old-fashioned alarm clock face up in a box. Dials are flat surfaces, round or rectangular, with an upright — miniature sundials, in fact, and much sought after, especially if in ivory. There are innumerable naval instruments, mainly concerned with navigation, and they mostly have a family resemblance, whether they are sextants, octants, or the rarer circumferentor.

There are also rarer instruments, designed for a variety of purposes such as measuring dewfall. In the main, these are rather dull. Balances come in all shapes and sizes, from the old-fashioned grocers' scales, often bought for decorative purposes, to precision-built chemists' and bankers' scales. If encased in a glass box, so much the better. Smaller precision scales, such as goldsmiths', are made to be carried in the pocket, and fold into a small box or case. Then there are one-offs, designed for arcane and mysterious pursuits; every dealer in scientific instruments has something in his shop that foxes him and his customers.

When purchasing any kind of instrument it is advisable to see if it works, making certain that *all* the lenses are intact and that any calibrating wheels are free. Discoloured brass can be brought up like new, and leather, often used in telescopes, can be replaced, if necessary by the cheaper leatherette. Replacement lenses can be made by grinding down old spectacle lenses (every junk shop has a box of old spectacles); not a job for a handyman, perhaps, but a jeweller or watchmaker will often oblige.

Sheet Music Covers

Print-making was revolutionized by the arrival of the process called lithography. For the first time it was possible to use large areas of colour in mass-produced pictures, and one of the industries that profited was music, particularly popular music. Music-hall songs were printed by the thousand, and many talented designers were recruited to provide a picture cover. There was also a big market in what was called salon music — music intended not for the concert hall but for home performance. Much of this music was sentimental, and gave great scope to the artists, many of whom came over from serious painting to enjoy the fruits of the commercial life.

Music-hall sheet music covers can be divided into two kinds — those with an illustration of the singer, and those depicting the

A high quality cover by Concanen, the top name in sheet music covers

subject of the song, which was often humorous or ironical. The most celebrated artist was Concanen, and his work is eagerly sought for, but there were many other illustrators who are still not collected.

The golden age of music covers was from about 1840 to 1890, when photography began to take over and it was considered that a photograph on the cover said more than any graphic artist could. For about thirty years music covers went into decline, even though the old lithographic techniques were taken up again. The colours were gaudy, the typography shoddy, and quality was sacrificed to quantity.

About 1920 a new school of artists backed by enterprising publishers began giving music covers a new image, using modern techniques and becoming more adventurous with their lay-out and typography, and many of these covers deserve to be rescued from oblivion. The coming of the talkies in the late 1920s was a disaster for the good artist. Songs from the films were published by the tens of thousands, and it was no longer necessary to attract a prospective buyer by means of a stylish cover. A single folded sheet was all that was needed, plus a photograph of the stars of the film.

In recent years, publishers of quality music such as Novello have begun to realize that a good cover adds to the sales appeal of the music, but popular music covers remain largely undistinguished, unlike record sleeves, which in some future decade must lend themselves to collecting.

Victorian lithographic covers are the most desirable, but the engraved covers which they supplanted are still neglected. Many of them are amateurish, done by jobbing artists for a few pence, but often they are interesting just on account of their quaintness. As many of the songs dealt with current topics they offer a unique sidelight on the age. Many of the engraved covers are 'half titles' – half the cover is a picture, half is the start of the music.

'Serious' music, meaning respectable music, disdained picture covers, and was content with words. They were words with a difference, however, spread over the cover and using different type faces and sizes until they dazzled the buyer. Sometimes there are as many as thirty different type faces on one cover, a designer's nightmare but impressive none the less. An enterprising collector could build up a definitive collection of typographical covers for under ten pounds.

Silver and Silver Plate

Fortunately for everyone, there are strict rules about silver, and the presence of a hallmark will normally give the authenticity of a piece. Normally, yes, but unscrupulous silversmiths have been known to graft the mark of a damaged or broken-up piece on to a more worthwhile specimen. However, this is not common.

Silver, as everyone knows, is an expensive material; articles that are old and large need a deep pocket to pay for them. Yet small pieces of silver are astonishingly cheap, often no more costly than the scrap value. For under ten pounds, sometimes a lot less than ten pounds, you can buy silver-backed brushes, silver-backed mirrors, napkin rings, silver-topped bottles, small containers, and every kind of nicknack, from silver toothpicks to silver thimbles. Odds and ends of cutlery in silver or part silver can be found in an antique shop cheaper than their fellows in plate in a chain store.

Dealers with long memories are nervous of silver. In 1968 it was $91\frac{1}{2}$p an ounce, due to a freak rise, but it was down to 57p an ounce by February 1972. It has risen again since then, and is now stable, keeping pace with inflation and is a reliable investment.

Foreigners are not so assiduous in marking silver as the British, and with unmarked items one has to take one's chance or use a kind of detection kit involving acids. Ambiguous items are described in sale catalogues as 'silver-coloured', a convenient let-out. It saves the embarrassment of misrepresentation, in particular calling silver plate silver.

Silver plate was a cheap substitute for silver. In the 1750s and 1760s silver was mechanically fused upon copper. This is Sheffield plate, and when the copper begins to show through the silver coating ('bleeding') it gives an attractive warm tinge. In 1844 electroplating was introduced; the silver was deposited on the base metal by chemical action. It was cheaper than Sheffield plate, and killed the old industry.

Sheffield plate *is* old, and is collected. Ordinary silver plate is not in itself interesting, though it is more versatile than Sheffield plate, the designers of which had to be careful, for cutting, deep engraving, or even sharp corners could mean the copper showing through and wrecking the illusion. The most common form of plating is EPNS (electroplated nickel silver) hardly magical symbols, for nickel silver is not even silver but an alloy of copper, nickel and zinc. Like stainless steel, EPNS serves a useful function but is otherwise worthless.

Silver plate can be confused with Britannia metal, a kind of pewter, which can also be plated. It was a popular metal for tea and coffee pots, as well as cutlery, and it has a dull look about it when the plating is beginning to wear off.

Smoking Accessories

Smoking accessories are often more interesting than the pipes themselves. They range from tobacco stoppers to tobacco jars, and although some of the items, such as novelty pipe-cleaners, are the kind of things wives buy as presents for pipe-smoking husbands, several types of accessories, such as vesta boxes, are very collectable.

The tobacco stopper is the object used to press down tobacco in the bowl to help the draw, and provides a most useful alternative to the gnarled finger. Stoppers were made of brass, bone, wood, bronze, pewter and silver, as well as substances that would frizzle if they came into contact with heat and thus condemn themselves as useless novelties. Tobacco stoppers are frequently mistaken for seals, and were often highly decorated, usually with such subjects as dogs or women's legs; they were sometimes combined with a metal or bone pricker, to break up clogged tobacco in the bowl.

Tobacco containers were made of wood, silver, glass, pottery, and sometimes lead; lead was used to line the casks, frequently in the form of barrels, though miniature coffins, egg-cups, urns, capstans and chess pieces all served as models. Tobacco containers can often be confused with tea-caddies, though a keyhole is a give-away — tea was very expensive and was locked away.

The manufacture of pipe-racks in fretwork was a highly popular do-it-yourself hobby, and they are sometimes incorporated in compendiums, either free-hanging or set up in a box called a smoker's cabinet. Every dealer at some time or other buys a smoker's cabinet and sells it three months later at the price he gave

An interesting advertisement for an elaborate smoker's tray. This was made as late as 1907 (*The Connoisseur*)

for it. They are usually stolidly made of oak and useless for any other purpose; so is a pipe-rack.

Lighting pipes (and cigarettes and cigars) was more interesting than storing them, and the vesta box was produced to contain matches that had a habit of bursting unaccountably into flames. The vesta itself was a type of match in which a wax taper was substituted for the familiar wooden stem. Vesta boxes were made in various materials, though brass, silver and silver plate were the most common. All vesta boxes had a serrated edge to strike the match on, and a secure lid with a foolproof catch (matches cannot self-ignite without air). Vesta boxes were sometimes fitted up with a small ring so that they could be attached to the owner's watch chain.

The earlier vesta boxes from the 1850s were modelled on snuff-boxes, but in the 1860s the lid was placed on the narrow side. As the century moved towards its close, a good deal of adventure went into designing vesta boxes, the only requirement being rounded corners (to avoid snagging pockets). There are boxes to be found in the form of hearts, bottles, elephants, pigs, half-moons, and fiddles, though the most common shape is the intricately chased rounded-off rectangle.

Silver, brass, and silver plate were first choices, but ivory, pottery, leather, mother-of-pearl, papier-mâché and celluloid were all used.

With the increasing use of boxed matches vesta boxes went into decline, but collectors of smoking accessories can turn to cigar and cigarette cases for fresh fields. Until the 1920s there was little enterprise in design – one leather or silver case looks very much like another – but the Art Deco designers using novel materials found opportunities for turning out modernistic, geometric, or simply quaint, cigarette boxes. There was also a fad for novelty boxes – intricate folding or slim boxes with a pop-up mechanism. Some of this gadgetry went into a new kind of smoking compendium incorporating cigarette box, lighter, and ashtray. Lighters date from World War I, but only in recent years have they been targets of fashionable aerospace designers.

One supposes that ashtrays come into the category of smoking accessories. Some early advertising ashtrays are worth getting hold of, but every seaside resort and every commemoration spawns so many wretched ashtrays that thinking people would rather collect rusty nails than lumber themselves with this particular accessory. But perhaps not.

Thimbles

At one time every antique shop had its crop of thimbles. Most of them were silver, and invariably had tiny holes in them which were not detected until the buyer got home. One silver thimble is very much like another one, and after acquiring a batch of them budding collectors went on to something with more variety though the assiduous looked further, discovering more out of the way examples.

Silver thimbles have been in use for several hundred years, but by the eighteenth century brass, iron, copper, ivory, bone, porcelain, gold, and wood were used. Many factories made porcelain thimbles (a Meissen thimble sold for £1,050 in 1970) often decorated with miniature paintings of birds, fruit and flowers and signed by the artist. They were quite rare until the mid-1960s when a sudden glut of them caused some rethinking. Prices went down from £20 overnight to a pound or two when it was realized that reproductions were about in quantity.

Enamel thimbles are even scarcer than old porcelain thimbles, and copies lie in wait for the unwary. Apart from reproductions meant to deceive, good quality enamel on silver thimbles are being made which do not pretend to be anything but brand new.

There is more fun in looking for advertising thimbles. These were often made from light metal so that they would emboss easily with the name of some product or other or a catchy slogan. There are also interesting adjustable thimbles, made to fit the finger of a growing child.

Pretty thimbles often form part of sets of sewing tools (*nécessaires*), and are frequently found encased in cases or holders, a favourite shape being an egg, either with a screw thread half-way down or having a hinged top. These eggs were made in a wide variety of materials such as wood, ivory, shagreen, leather, tortoiseshell, gold, silver, and brass. An acorn was another popular shape, and actual nut shells were used, hinged and lined. For the very prestigious jobs, nut-shell cases contained miniature sewing tools, occasionally of gold.

The great advantage of a collection of thimbles is that they can be beautifully displayed in a small space. A new collector should, however, take care not to accumulate very ordinary battered silver thimbles, which are not worth much more than their scrap value.

Tiles

Tiles are small, usually inexpensive, and can be displayed to good effect. They have a tendency to get 'nibbled', usually because they are difficult to remove from their setting without damage. They have been used for flooring, mural and ceiling decoration, picture panels, built into fireplaces, mantelpieces, and furniture.

Among the most interesting are the early 'encaustic' tiles used for flooring. An encaustic tile is a decorative glazed and fired tile, having patterns of different coloured clays inlaid in it and burnt with it. These can date from the thirteenth century, and are being faked. Their usual colouring was yellowy-white against red or chocolate for British tiles, which were less colourful than those from Spain and Italy. These were in turn less lavish than eastern tiles, which were often made in large slabs, modelled in relief with passages from sacred books or names and dates of rulers. The Italians and the Spanish brought in colourful painted tiles, but in Britain the blue and white tiles from the Netherlands proved more popular, leading to English makers at Lambeth, Liverpool and Bristol jumping on the band-waggon. Blue and white, both in pottery and tiles, was an international style.

Early blue and white tiles were one-offs, often quaint, always delightful, and it is difficult to say where they came from. Transfer-printing in the eighteenth century brought the pretty tile to the people; in about 1830 a patent was granted for the manufacture of tiles by mechanical means, a patent purchased in 1844 by Minton and a Worcester firm, which sold its stock to John Maw in 1850. By the end of the century Maw & Co was the biggest tile company in the world, though never rivalling Minton in prestige.

Mass-production methods improved, and Doulton made stoneware tiles, which were unaffected by the elements, for the

A group of fine Delft tiles (*Victoria & Albert Museum*)

exterior of buildings. Many are still there, as good as new. The Gothic Revival provided a spur to the manufacturers of ecclesiastical tiles for new churches, often encaustic tiles in the old style. The compression of powdered clay made possible a vast variety of decorative tiles, and high-quality potters employed skilled designers for 'limited editions'.

Butchers, dairies, refreshment rooms, railway stations, private houses, all contained acres of tiles. The coming of linoleum in 1860 cut down the use of floor tiling, but there was still plenty of work for the manufacturers, some of which employed 2,000 workers and had a production capacity of half a million tiles a week.

The decorative devices of *art nouveau* were well suited to the tile and the lotus and the lily, the curls and swirls, were everywhere.

95

For the best in *art nouveau* tiling go to Harrod's meat hall of 1902, where the tiles can still be seen.

After World War I tiles were *infra dig*, and although a few art potters made some none are of striking interest. Do-it-yourself has brought the tile back again; an old tile in a bathroom wall or in a kitchen can be very effective, as can imitation old tiles. Reproduction Delft blue and white is the most popular line, and a nibbled edge and a crack or two are more welcome than they were. Modern manufacturers have not yet caught on to the possibilities of producing damaged goods.

Tins

The ready availability of tinplate transformed the toy industry, and created a packaging revolution towards the end of the nineteenth century, though the earliest known biscuit tin dates from the 1860s. A general lapse of patents in 1889 opened the door to all kinds of adventurous design, and tins were produced in a huge variety of shapes and sizes.

The main aim was to make a tin box look like something else, following a nineteenth-century trend in which cast iron was disguised as wood and, if need be, wood was disguised as cast iron.

A novelty tin of unusual design (*The Picture Magazine*)

Some of the substances had proved intractable, but tin was ideal, as it could be twisted and contorted into any shape and took a design well. So we have tins in the form of birds, chests of drawers, handbags, Chinese vases, or, the favourite, a library of books, a dodge that came in about 1900.

The cleverest work was done on biscuit tins, not because biscuits were especially suitable for fancy packaging but because Huntley and Palmer were pioneers in exploiting the possibilities of tin. The manufacturers of sweets and chocolates were also responsible for pretty boxes; they were luxury items for which the seller did not mind spending a few coppers over for the tin. Tobacco was also packed in tins, but the manufacturers did not exert themselves too much over design. After all, men were not interested in the fripperies, only in whether or not the container was air-tight. It was considered that biscuit and sweet tins had woman-appeal and, increasingly important, child-appeal.

Apparently they did, and still have for unusual tins can fetch silly prices, particularly in London. The provincial collector has proved more circumspect, and out of town dealers often have a surplus of tins gathering rust and dust.

Toys

There is a wealth of variety in old toys. Some categories have been taken up by collectors but there remains virgin territory for a newcomer to conquer where prices are fixed by supply and demand and there is no tiresome price-guide to lay down hard and fast rules.

Until the eighteenth century toys were little regarded, and quickly cast aside. Poor children were contented with roughly carved billets of wood that would serve any purpose, while the children of the rich were hurried through their childhood so that they could become little adults. Simple teaching toys such as alphabet blocks were used in the home and in dame-schools, and many of the eighteenth-century toys that have survived were educational. There were more frivolous toys such as cut-outs in paper and card, including paper dolls that were 'dressed' with interchangeable units.

Towards the end of the eighteenth century flat metal toys in relief were made in Germany, and Nuremberg began to establish itself as a key toy-making centre. Tin soldiers proved an early favourite, as was miniature cooking ware. Such toys were extremely basic, but the coming of the clockwork motor in the 1880s gave much more scope to the makers. There was a duty on mechanical toys according to weight – one of the reasons why tinplate toys are fragile and easily dented. By simple systems of gearing, tin toys could do many things; there were bucking mules and people jumping up and down.

Frivolous toys competed with educational toys throughout the nineteenth century. Board-games promoted the learning of geography, history, science and, particularly, scripture. Many were on the snakes-and-ladders principle. The jigsaw puzzle was invented by a firm of map-makers in the 1760s. They were called 'Dissected Maps' – the jigsaw was the instrument which cut them. There were no intricate shapes, and not many pieces, and they made few demands on the bright child, who was catered for by 'philosophical' toys such as the Thaumatrope (about 1826), the Zoetrope (1832), and the Praxinoscope (1878). All these marvels depended on the phenomenon of the persistence of vision, and the basic ingredient was viewing through a slit of aperture a succession of pictures, each one slightly different so that movement was suggested.

Magic lanterns were cheap and tinny (for children) or expensive and precision-made (for adults). Movement was simulated by trick slides, which were jogged in the frame or passed in succession quickly through the slide slot to give some animation. Animals and people rolling their eyes was a favourite trick.

The paper cut-outs of the eighteenth century were improved on for the toy theatre. About 1811 pictures of actors and scenery were printed on to sheets, were cut out in the home and mounted on card, and then placed in a miniature theatre. The actors and actresses were moved about in response to the action. Peepshows were the same kind of thing, miniature panoramas made from card and paper. By looking through a hole, a peepshow gave an impression of perspective; adults had their own peepshows, called dioramas, just as they had their own card games. Children had 'Snap' and 'Happy Families', as well as more ephemeral card games.

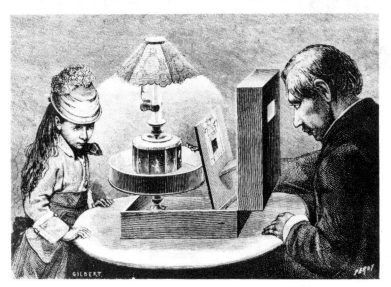

The praxinoscope, an optical toy of about 1880 (*Science Museum*)

Time has been hard on many toys. Tin is amenable to rust, and card and paper becomes tatty. Fortunately some of the most collectable toys were made of sterner stuff – the lead of model soldiers, a category promoted in Great Britain by a man named Britain, who was well able to counter the Nuremberg toy-makers. The collectors of militaria, renowned for their enthusiasm, have moved into the toy soldier market, pushing the prices up. Not that lead soldiers are very old – the process was patented by William Britain in 1893.

However, toys do not have to be ancient to be desirable. The tin toys of the 1920s and 1930s have their enthusiasts, and their more robust contemporaries – the Hornby trains – regularly turn up at Sotheby's collectors' sales. A less widely publicized toy is making considerable headway – the Dinky toy, and the vehicles of the 1950s immortalized in miniature appear as interesting as the real life Ford or Jaguar, and often more so.

The most favoured tin toys are those representing specific objects, such as the airship R 101. Painted tin toys are usually older than those where the decoration is applied paper designs. Most are unmarked though the patent letters D.R.G.M. or D.R.P. indicate that they are of German origin, while F.M. is the mark of the best-known French maker Fernand Martin. The German firm of Lehman (founded 1851) often marked their products fully, but Bing (founded 1863) is thought of more highly. G.B.N. indicates a Bing toy pre-1919, B.W. after 1919.

It may require an effort of will to see a penny toy as an antique, but the boom in nostalgia can make an antique of even the most unlikely object.

Walking Sticks

Walking sticks of all types are not at all expensive, even when they have silver tops and ferrules, and the country stick with perhaps a century of use behind it and another century's wear in it can cost no more than the imitation shepherd's crook sold in a gift shop. The Rolls-Royces of walking sticks are the 'dandy' sticks, usually in a hard wood, long, and beautifully made. They are similar in appearance to the batons used by drum-majorettes in processions. A collection of walking sticks can be surprisingly appealing, for they come in a variety of shapes and woods.

However, there is no question that ordinary walking sticks are less interesting than dual purpose sticks, the best-known of which is the sword-stick, which dates back at least to the sixteenth century and was brought into being by town ordinances forbidding the wearing of swords. The most simple type, widely reproduced today, is a straight-forward rapier sliding into a cane, but other blades were released by spring catches. Sometimes there was more than one blade. There was also a telescopic javelin concealed in a cane, measuring 9ft when extruded.

The poacher's gun was a genuine concealed weapon, simple but effective; it was used not for the pursuit of the poacher's trade but as a defence against gamekeepers when nineteenth-century game laws were sternly applied and punishments were horrendous. Sometimes a harmless looking cane concealed a pistol or a revolver.

The shooting stick is a common enough object; the handle adjusts to form a seating surface. But during the nineteenth century nearly a hundred patents were taken out for more elaborate seats, with two, three, or four legs. There was also a patent taken out for a walking stick that could be converted into a ladder; one writer on walking sticks suggests that this was for the use of Peeping Toms, but in fact it was for escaping from mad dogs during a particular hydrophobia scare. There are also walking sticks that convert into photographers' tripods, painters' easels, music stands, and even lecterns for peripatetic preachers.

Walking sticks also contained tuning forks, conductor's batons, pipes (for tobacco or opium), cigarettes and cigars, but the most ingenuity was applied to providing small items in the handles where the handle becomes nothing more than a small box. Everything that could conceivably be put into a small space can be found in a cane handle – vesta boxes, musical boxes, snuff boxes, cigarette lighters, vinaigrettes, or even coins.

Some of the more common things contained in canes are corkscrews, mirrors, maps, parasols, pencils, whistles, measuring sticks (for surveyors and architects), billiard cues (in two sections), fishing rods, and drinking glasses. Victorian sex maniacs had canes with a mirror by the ferrule to look under ladies' skirts.

A walking stick which is not a walking stick is a pocket violin, very much collected by specialists, which fits into a small container a mere two inches in diameter. This is not a child's toy, but a serious instrument used by itinerant violinists and music teachers.

So an ordinary looking walking stick may well spring a surprise on a diligent browser.

Witch Balls

There are few novice dealers who have not bought a fishing float under the impression that it was a witch ball. In fact, anything which is spherical and has no obvious reason to exist is called a witch ball, when it could easily be something else, such as a reflecting globe. These were glass spheres lustred to resemble silver, which were placed in dark rooms to add light. Early reflecting globes were imported from the continent, but from about 1690 English examples in tough clear glass appeared. The silvering method was rough and ready, creating distortions in the reflections, but a process was discovered in 1843 in which the mercury of the older types was replaced by real silver, which gave a yellow tinge.

These lustred globes were never really successful as the lustre was damaged by the climate, but a solution was found in which one globe was set inside a slightly larger one, the gap being filled with silver, and the double globe sealed. These reflecting globes were always expensive. The true witch ball was really a spherical bottle holding holy water. It was hung up to drive away evil, and the bottle was wiped every day to remove any nasty residues that may have accumulated overnight.

Most of these bottles were dark green in colour, but towards the end of the eighteenth century blue glass was used, and scriptural texts were applied in gold. Spherical globes were made in the early nineteenth century in various colours, but these did not have apertures, and are said to be jug covers to keep out dust and insects. Whatever they are, they are very decorative and worth buying, though it would be wrong to suggest that there are enough of them about to build up a collection.

4 Investing in Antiques

This is a polite way of saying 'Making money out of antiques'. And why not? The British are not only a nation of shopkeepers, but a nation of buyers and sellers. Let us take pleasure in turning over an honest penny.

True antiques will always appreciate in value; pseudo-antiques are not so certain. The question to be answered is what is a pseudo-antique, for there is an area where trendy bits and pieces merge into true collectables. One should always be suspicious of items which are reproduced for a modern demand, a demand often fostered by Sunday newspaper supplements. Two characteristic examples are *art nouveau* posters and Lowry prints.

Anything which is the product of craftsmanship is worth acquiring, from a piece of Sheraton furniture to a sheet music cover designed by Concanen. The way a thing is made can be judged by non-experts better than its age or its value. A good question to ask oneself is whether, if one had the time and the facilities at hand, one could make it. The answer if faced with a fretwork nineteenth-century pipeholder is, if one had a fretsaw, decidedly yes. Could you make a skeleton clock, an elaborate Edwardian inlaid sideboard, a nineteenth-century plate camera, even if you had the right tools? If you could, you are wasting your time reading this book. You should be busy in your workshop making a million.

It is all very well to jump on some band-waggon or other, and the snag is trying to jump on it when it has passed by. There will always be someone who recognizes that something is under-rated; if he is a dealer he will build up a quiet collection, and then release whatever it is on to the market. The most profitable way to do this is at auction. The dealer will bid up his own goods; it does not matter at this stage if they do not sell or if he is obliged to buy them in. The fact that a Victorian left-handed spooning iron (don't look for one – they don't exist) has reached a record figure in an auction will be registered, and those unaware that they have been cunningly worked on will rush around trying to buy them up. Willing allies will be found in writers on antiques in the antique magazines,

🎵HE 🎵ODAK

Is the smallest, lightest, and simplest of all Detective Cameras—for the ten operations necessary with most Cameras of this class to make one exposure, we have **only 3 simple** movements.

NO FOCUSSING.   NO FINDER REQUIRED.

Size 3¼ by 3¾ by 6½ inches.   **MAKES 100 EXPOSURES.**   Weight 35 ounces.

Setting the Shutter.

Exposing.

Winding more Film.

Cutting off Exposure.

Removing the Roller Slide.

Drawing off Exposed Films.

Cutting off Exposures.

Developing 12 at once.

Placing New Roll of 100 in position.

Placing Film in Roller Slide.

Examining Negatives (three on one strip).

Complete Kodak.

Carrying Case.

FULL INFORMATION FURNISHED BY

THE EASTMAN DRY PLATE & FILM Co., 115, Oxford St., London, W.

The kind of early Kodak that can make up to a hundred pounds (*Science Museum*)

104

A classic piece of furniture which inevitably appreciates in value (*Magazine of Art*)

the Sundays, or the better quality women's magazines, if only for the reason that all the 'standards' have been covered and writers on antiques are desperate to find new things to chat about.

It is a matter of dispute as to whether we have reached the limit on fine Victorian furniture; it seems difficult to envisage it going any higher. It is a solid investment, as it won't fall in value, but some of the prices now are fantastic compared with those obtained in the mid-1960s. In summer 1977 a battered Victorian ladies' chair that a dealer at the auction said he would have burned ten years

A magnificent piece of Victoriana. One could pay *anything* for this and be sure of a profit in a year's time (*Art Journal*)

ago made £320 in a matter of minutes. A Victorian brass bed fetched £495 – a quality brass bed with side screens, but only a brass bed. An ordinary rosewood work box made £100, and a walnut chest-of-drawers made £560 (something of a freak figure). Even a pair of Victorian wire pot-plant holders realized £138.

Edwardian furniture is decidedly worth buying as an investment, but there are indications that fine pieces fetch fine prices. At an auction in Nantwich in July 1977 a disguised drink cabinet in inlaid mahogany, Regency style, made £560, surprising the auctioneers who put an estimate on it of £200–£300. The quality of Edwardian cabinet-making is now recognized, and inlaid mahogany furniture of the period is worth looking out for. If you make a mistake and buy genuine Regency rather than reproduction Regency you are decidedly on the winning side – it is a game you cannot lose.

In pottery and porcelain there are certain categories which must be over the top. It is difficult to know why, for example, Goss

The kind of bisque figures one could pick up for a few shillings ten years ago. Bisque is still underpriced

miniatures have rocketed in value; Goss did make some excellent porcelain, but the miniatures, the armorial pieces, were never more than sixpenny and shilling touches. Certainly it is not the miniaturization that has the appeal, for other potteries turning out miniatures are well nigh ignored, even when their products are identical to those of Goss. It may be that small urns, cottages, etc are picked out in a crowded shop and it is a matter of seconds to turn them over for the magic trademark.

Pot-lids were originally throwaway items, but have proved enormously popular not only with serious collectors but the general public. A great deal of research has been carried out, pot-lids being honoured with a price-guide at an early stage and with the subsequent attentions of the reproducer.

A good way to get into the collecting of pottery and porcelain is to concentrate on the products of one firm, such as Royal Doulton or, preferably, the admirable Midwinter pottery which did some striking work in the 1930s, work that is largely unrecognized. Even fine Doulton plates with a fair bit of age to them can be picked up for less than five pounds. More readily displayed than plates are figurines, and even fairly recent examples (such as Churchill) have appreciated ten times since they were moulded in the 1960s. The products of the art potteries are well worth collecting if one has a feel for them and genuinely likes them, though a thin line divides art potteries from commercial potteries. Devon is deluged under Watcombe pottery which, in theory at least, was an art pottery.

Collecting can become an obsession, and the zeal with which some people go at it can be off-putting. A book could be filled with off-beat categories, and who is to decide whether, say, *Eagle* comics are a 'proper' thing to collect when the collectors of *Magnet* are most assuredly a respectable bunch? The postcard specialists who dote over the cards designed by Louis Wain and Donald McGill are not regarded as freaks, so why should those who prefer postcards depicting cricketers and who write all over the world for them? Looking for such exalted ephemera can be another form of investment. One buys cheaply from those who do not reckon them, and sells expensively to those who do.

What is a cast-iron certainty? First of all, anything of quality

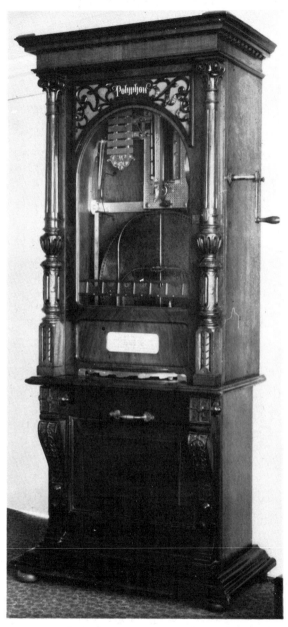

Ten years ago it was unthinkable for a Polyphon to make £1,000. Now the £2,000 barrier has been broken, but that is still not too much for such a splendid piece of machinery (*Graham Webb*)

that has not been through a dealer's hands. Secondly, the 'classics' of whatever age. Thirdly, articles intrinsically valuable, such as precious stones, silver, and gold. Not forgetting platinum. Still, it is more fun speculating in the fringe area, provided that one does not come in at the tail-end of a trend.

An umbrella stand in cast iron, a medium still largely unappreciated (*Art Journal*)

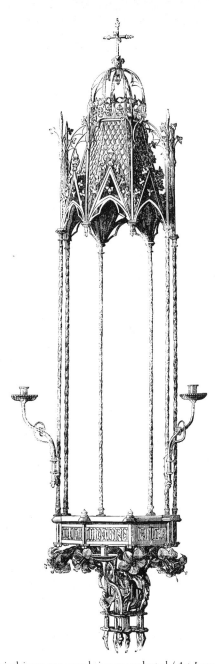

Vaguely ecclesiastical items are now being re-evaluated (*Art Journal*)

Here is a list of fifteen categories still wide open to the observant:

Anything made of gold
Art Deco jewellery
Art Deco pottery and porcelain, especially 'novelty' items
Enamel buttons, brooches, and tokens – anything fixed to a dress or lapel
Etchings
Large Victorian dinner services
Miniature and doll's house furniture
Porcelain miniatures *not* by Goss
Portrait busts in pottery, porcelain, wood and metal
Quality furniture of the 1920s and 1930s
Small silver articles
Sporting prints
Victorian cast iron
Victorian costume jewellery
Wrought iron

Appendix 1 Recent Prices at Auction

It should be noted that auction prices *can* be misleading, and an astonishing figure can be produced by two keen bidders throwing caution to the wind. A low figure may mean that the dealers' ring is in operation, artificially keeping the price low; there is no way of knowing this from auction records.

	£
Act of Parliament Clock by Hawkins, 1730	1,200
Art Deco geometric clock by Preisse in marble and onyx	260
Art Deco table lighter and cigarette holder, negro barman shaking a cocktail	75
Art Deco wireless set, round, in wood with chrome facings c 1930	110
Art nouveau bronze table lamp with draped female figure	130
Art nouveau enamelled glass pitcher by Gallé	1,120
Art nouveau silver belt buckle by Liberty's 1902	60
Art nouveau silvered metal mirror with naked female figure	360
Bing clockwork locomotive and tender c 1900	48
Biscuit barrel with silver lid, two handles	175
Black Cat cigarette poster in metal	35
Bran tub fairground machine c 1940	18
Brass bound oval rum cask	30
Brass roasting jack	21
Brass sextant by Carey of London, early nineteenth century	85
Brass spirit kettle	30
Bristol Delft blue and white charger	50
Clarice Cliff 'Bizarre' pattern charger, 1930s	50
Claudet cased daguerreotype stereoscope with six portraits	520
Clockwork toys (sixteen) by Schuco and Triang	193
Collection of twenty-four spectacles and lorgnettes	70
Copper jelly mould	24
Copper warming pan	56
Coronation coach with horses, made by Britains, early twentieth century	50

Dinky toys (eleven) (motor-cars)	195
Dutch Delft charger depicting William of Orange	300
Edison home phonograph Model A (1896–1901) with thirty cylinders	190
Edwardian breakfront bookcase	630
Edwardian breakfront bookcase 9ft high	2,600
Edwardian gilt and white ten-piece dining-room suite	2,600
Edwardian inlaid rosewood credenza	200
Eighteenth-century Derby punchbowl	720
Eighteenth-century walnut and elm dresser base in poor condition	870
Famille rose dinner-service of 286 pieces	16,000
Fifteen-piece Mason's part dinner-service	95
Four framed panels of Chinese wallpaper	720
George V Jubilee biscuit tin (1935)	16
Georgian mahogany deed box with brass handles	14
Georgian mahogany knife box with serpentine front and inlay of satinwood	38
Georgian oak linen press	300
Georgian oval gilt mirror with swags	500
Goss model of Selgrave Manor	780
Goss model of Thomas Hardy's house	80
Ivory netsuke in shape of grotesque mask	120
Ivory netsuke in shape of three boys around bowl	270
Japanese lacquered and decorated ostrich egg with ivory top	450
Jigsaw puzzle of Great Exhibition of 1851	52
Kodak roll-film camera of c 1890	120
Large ammonite fossil	22
Large copper fish pan	76
Large copper preserving pan	52
Large Lyons Dundee fruit cake tin 1952 with original c ke	8
Mucha litho panel 'Iris'	200
Musical snuffbox playing four operatic airs	210
Nineteenth-century brass lantern clock	105
Nineteenth-century carved oak hallstand in shape of bear	750
Nineteenth-century marine barometer by Morton of Glasgow	650

Nineteenth-century writing slope with brass inlay and ivory knobs	34
Nineteenth-century zither	20
Oak roll-top desk	150
Oak three-bottle tantalus	72
Octagonal table in satinwood in Ecclesiastical style designed by Pugin	460
Orange tree musical automaton	90,000
Pair Venetian nineteenth-century blackamoor marble busts	32,000
Pair Bristol blue glass decanters with copper collars	95
Pair Chippendale style pole screens	1,100
Pair nineteenth-century jockey scales	250
Pair cut glass square decanters with silver mounts 1903	95
Pair Victorian Chinese Chippendale display cabinets	700
Penny-farthing bicycle c 1870	400
Polyphon, standing type	2,000
Posters, 160 circus and music-hall	600
Propeller with clock in centre	14
Queen Anne oak food cupboard with slatted top	1,100
Reflecting telescope by Tulley of Islington	500
Regency sycamore tea caddy with brass lions' mask handles	11
Remington noiseless typewriter c 1925	16
Rolls-Royce mascot 'Spirit of Ecstasy' 1907	100
Ruskin mauve and green vase 1906	74
Sampler dated 1831	105
Satsuma barrel-shaped cricket cage	310
Scrap album of 1870s containing 150 nude photographs	80
Set of twenty-seven Grenadier Guards lead soldiers	30
Seventeenth-century green bottle with initials WM	210
Shell hand-operated petrol pump c 1935	130
Sikes hydrometer late nineteenth century	38
Silk Tabriz rug depicting tree of life supporting bird and cage	8,000
Silver tankard made by William Shaw, reign of George III, weight 27oz	1,050

Only a poster, but posters now make money (*Victoria & Albert Museum*)

Silver thimble c 1850 with representation of Royal Pavilion	32
Six Chippendale style mahogany dining chairs, four singles and two carvers, c 1890	430
Staffordshire flat figures of two cricketers	460
Stereo daguerreotype of woman by Claudet	130
Stevenograph of Queen Victoria and family	400
Stuffed white pheasant	20
Teak ship's wheel	95
Three Fulham pottery tiles designed by Morgan	220
Three ivory tusks weighing 11½lb	130
Tiger skin rug	120
Tiffany glass blue lustre vase with frilled rim and applied drops	210
Two low Chinese rosewood tables	160
2lb of horsehair (for repairing violin bows)	38
Victorian apothecaries' drug jar	120
Victorian coffee-bean grinder	85
Victorian credenza	170
Victorian mahogany Chesterfield	210
Victorian loo table in burr walnut	540
Victorian silver grape scissors	58
Victorian silver hand-bell	260
Victorian umbrella stand in cast iron	35
Victorian walnut Davenport	450
Victorian wicker bath-chair	20
Violin by John Betts dated 1792	950
'What the Butler Saw' machine 1920–30	250
William III silver candlesticks, a pair, dated 1698	600
Wooden drum from Sandwich Islands	62,000
Wurlitzer juke box of 1946	1,900

Appendix 2 Antique Markets

It must be mentioned that antique markets come and go without apparent rhyme or reason. Sometimes it is fluctuation in trade, sometimes markets go under during the bad months of January and February, and sometimes it is simply a question of bad organization. Occasionally organizers misjudge the trade, charge too much for their stalls, and dealers with expensive pretty bits stand about all day while the visitors browse but do not buy.

Generally speaking, the one day markets are the true markets. The stall-holders have to take their money there and then and do not hold out for silly prices. In markets open every day, the stall holders usually live in the locality; for one day markets, the stall holders sometimes travel a considerable distance, often as much as sixty or seventy miles. With travelling time and petrol expenses, they are not there for their health.

The Shipyard, River Rd, ARUNDEL, Sussex	Sat
Guinea Lane, Paragon, BATH, Avon	Wed
Corn Exchange, Corn St, BRISTOL, Avon	Fri
26–28 The Mall, Clifton, BRISTOL, Avon	Tues–Sat
St John's Hall, Whiteladies Rd, BRISTOL, Avon	Mon
Maltings Rd, BATTLESBRIDGE, Essex	Wed–Sun
The Green (on A30) BATTLESBRIDGE, Essex	Wed–Sun
Church Hall, Edison Rd, BROMLEY, Kent	Sat
United Reformed Church Halls, Widmore Rd, BROMLEY, Kent	Thurs
St Paul's Parochial Hall, Newnham St, BOLTON, Lancs	Thurs
Blackpool Pleasure Beach, BLACKPOOL, Lancs	Sun
Quakers' Mill, Old Town, BEXHILL, Sussex	Mon–Sun
41 Meeting House Lane, BRIGHTON, Sussex	Mon–Sat
St Martin's Market, Edgbaston St, BIRMINGHAM, Warwicks	Mon
141 Bromsgrove St, BIRMINGHAM, Warwicks	Thurs
St Peter's Place, Broad St, BIRMINGHAM, Warwicks	Thurs, Sun
Scout Hall, Silver Hill, CHALFONT ST GILES, Bucks	First Wed in month
Guildhall, CHARD, Somerset	Thurs
54 Suffolk St, CHELTENHAM, Glos	Mon–Sat
12 St Mary's St, CHEPSTOW, Gwent	Mon–Sat

Guildhall, Watergate St, CHESTER	Thurs
Corn Hall, Market Place, CIRENCESTER, Glos	Fri
7 Trinity St, COLCHESTER, Essex	Mon, Tues, Thurs, Fri, Sat
Red Cross Centre, Lower Chantry Lane, CANTERBURY, Kent	Sat
Memorial Hall, High St, CODICOTE, Herts	First Sat in month
St Peter's Hall, Ledbury Rd, SOUTH CROYDON, Surrey	Fri
Eagle Centre, DERBY	Sat
Nanteos Mansions, nr ABERYSTWYTH, Dyfed, Wales	First Mon in month (summer)
80 Seaside, EASTBOURNE, Sussex	Mon–Sat
St Stephen's St, EDINBURGH	Mon–Sat
79 High St, ETON, Berks	Tues–Sat
3 Church St, FINEDON, Northants	Mon–Sat
178a Bath St, GLASGOW	Mon–Sat
67 West Regent St, GLASGOW	Mon–Sat
22 Haydon Place, GUILDFORD, Surrey	Tues, Thurs, Fri, Sat
High St, GREAT MISSENDEN, Bucks	Mon, Tues, Wed, Fri, Sat
Piece Hall, HALIFAX, Yorks	Fri
Battinson Rd, HALIFAX, Yorks	Thurs–Sat
St George, HARROGATE, Yorks	Thurs
27 High St, HEATHFIELD, Sussex	Mon, Tues, Wed, Thurs, Sat
High St, HUNGERFORD, Berks	Mon–Sat
Cromwell House, Kimbolton, HUNTINGDON, Cambs	Tues–Sun
Abbey Hotel, KENILWORTH, Warwicks	Mon
High St, KIDWORTH BEAUCHAMP, Leics	Tues–Sat
14 Broad St, LEOMINSTER, Herefordshire	Wed–Fri
Guildford Rd, LEATHERHEAD, Surrey	Mon–Sun
United Reform Church Hall, Market Hill, MALDON, Essex	First Sat in month
10a King St West, MANCHESTER	Mon–Sat
High St, MARLBOROUGH, Wilts	Mon–Sat
Knockhundred Row, MIDHURST, Sussex	Mon–Sat
Market Place, NEWARK, Notts	Mon–Sat
Bartholomew St, NEWBURY, Berks	Mon, Tues, Thurs, Fri, Sat
55 East St, NEWTON ABBOT, Devon	Tues
Civic Hall, Hinderton Rd, NESTON, Cheshire	Last Sat of month
39 Sheep St, NORTHAMPTON	Mon–Sat
St Andrews Hall, George St, NORWICH, Norfolk	Wed
Angel St, PETWORTH, Sussex	Mon–Fri

Barbican, PLYMOUTH, Devon	Mon–Sat
Drake Circus, PLYMOUTH, Devon	Mon–Sat
Merchants Place, READING, Berks	Mon–Sat
Cinque Port St, RYE, Sussex	Thurs and Sat
Strand House, RYE, Sussex	Mon–Sun
Cattle Market, ST COLUMB MAJOR, Cornwall	Fri
High St, SANDGATE, Kent	Mon–Sun
Church Lane, SEAFORD, Sussex	Mon, Thurs, Sat
Setts Market, SHEFFIELD, Yorks	Mon
High St, SKIPTON, Yorks	Sun
120 London Rd, SEVENOAKS, Kent	Mon–Sat
Bligh Hotel, High St, SEVENOAKS, Kent	Wed
93 High St, STEYNING, Sussex	Sat
78 Church St, TEWKESBURY, Glos	Tues and Sat
Barrington St, TIVERTON, Devon	Mon, Tues, Wed, Fri, Sat
7 Little Castle St, TRURO, Cornwall	Mon, Tues, Wed, Fri, Sat
32 High St, Rusthall, TUNBRIDGE WELLS, Kent	Mon–Sat
176 High St, UCKFIELD, Sussex	Mon–Sat
St John's Church Hall, Royal Lane, UXBRIDGE, Middx	Second Sat in month
20–22 High St, WARWICK	Mon, Tues, Wed, Fri, Sat
King's Walk, WINCHESTER, Hants	Mon, Tues, Wed, Fri, Sat
Woburn Abbey, WOBURN, Beds	Mon–Sun

London Antique Markets

Even more than provincial markets, London markets are subject to the laws of supply and demand. The following are more or less well established.

Alfie's, Church St, NW8	Tues, Wed, Thurs, Fri, Sat
Antiquarius, 135–143 King's Rd, SW3	Mon–Sat
Antique Hypermarket, Kensington High St, W8	Mon–Sat
Antique Supermarket, behind Selfridges, W1	Mon–Sat
Bayswater, 132 Bayswater Rd, W2	Sun, Mon, Tues, Wed, Fri
Bond St Centre, 111–112 New Bond St, W1	Mon–Sat
Caledonian Market, Bermondsey, SE1	Fri morning

Camberwell Antique Market, 159–161 Camberwell Rd, SE1	Thurs, Fri, Sun
Camden Lock, Camden Rd, NW1	Mon–Sun
Camden Passage, Islington, N1	Wed, Sat
Charing Cross, WC2	Mon–Sat
Chelsea Antiques Market, 245a and 253 King's Rd, SW3	Mon–Sat
Crawford Antiques Market, 43 Craven St, W1	Mon–Fri
Earl's Court Market, Car Park Exhibition Hall, W5	Sun
Ebury Antique Centre, 199–203 Buckingham Palace Rd, SW1	Mon–Sat
Hampstead Antiques, 12 Heath St, NW3	Tues–Sat
Hampstead Market, High St, NW6	Thurs
Marylebone Market, 43 Crawford St, W1	Mon–Sat
'Up the Market', 22 Shorts Gardens, WC2	Mon–Sat
Petticoat Lane, E1 (Petticoat Lane is the name given to the whole complex of streets)	Sun
Portobello Rd, W11	Sat (though the shops in the road are open every day)

Bibliography

Except where stated the following books are published in London.

Andere, M.	*Old Needlework Boxes and Tools* (David & Charles 1971; Newton Abbot)
Ash, D.	*Dictionary of British Antique Silver* (Pelham 1972)
Barilli, R.	*Art Nouveau* (Hamlyn) 1969
Battersby, M.	*The Decorative Twenties* (Studio Vista 1970)
	The Decorative Thirties (Studio Vista 1972)
Bedford, J.	*Victorian Prints* (Cassell 1969)
Bemrose, G.	*Nineteenth-Century English Pottery and Porcelain* (Faber 1952)
Boger, L. A.	*Complete Guide to Furniture Styles* (Black 1961)
	Dictionary of World Pottery and Porcelain (Black 1972)
Britten, F. J.	*Old Clocks and Watches* (Eyre Methuen 1894)
Cowie, D. & Henshaw, K.	*Antique Collectors' Dictionary* (Arco 1962)
Coysh, A. W.	*Blue and White Transfer Ware 1780–1840* (David & Charles 1970; Newton Abbot)
	British Art Pottery (David & Charles 1976; Newton Abbot)
Elville, E. M.	*Paperweights* (Country Life 1954)
Evans, J.	*A History of Jewellery 1100–1870* (Faber 1953)
Fastnedge, R.	*English Furniture Style 1500–1830* (Penguin 1955)
Fleming, J. & Honour, H.	*Penguin Dictionary of Decorative Arts* (Penguin 1977)
Flower, M.	*Victorian Jewellery* (Cassell 1951)
Gloag, J. E.	*Short Dictionary of Furniture* (Allen & Unwin 1954)
Godden, G. A.	*British Pottery and Porcelain 1780–1850* (Barrie & Jenkins 1963)
	Encyclopaedia of British Pottery and Porcelain Marks (Barrie & Jenkins 1964)
Gorden, H.	*Antiques – the Amateur's Questions* (Murray 1951)
Gray, B.	*The English Print* (Black 1937)
Haggar, R. G.	*English Country Pottery* (Phoenix House 1950)
Hayward, H. (ed)	*Handbook of Antique Collecting* (Connoisseur 1960)
Hillier, B.	*Art Deco of the 20s and 30s* (Studio Vista 1968)
Honey, W. B.	*Dictionary of European Ceramic Art* (Faber 1952)
Hughes, B. & T.	*Small Antique Furniture* (Lutterworth 1958)
Kendrick, A. F.	*English Needlework* (Black 1933)
Lloyd, A.	*Chats on Old Clocks* (Benn 1951)
Oman, C. C.	*English Domestic Silver* (Black 1959)
Osborne, H. (ed)	*Oxford Companion to the Decorative Arts* (OUP 1975)

Pearsall, R.	*Collecting Mechanical Antiques* (David & Charles 1973; Newton Abbot)
	Collecting and Restoring Scientific Instruments (David & Charles 1974; Newton Abbot)
Pevsner, N.	*Industrial Art in England* (CUP 1937)
Pinto, E. H.	*Treen* (Batsford 1949)
Ramsay, L. G. G. (ed)	*Concise Encyclopaedia of Antiques* (Connoisseur 1956)
Read, H.	*Art and Industry* (Faber 1945)
Ridley, M. J.	*Oriental Art* (Gifford 1970)
Rogers, J. C.	*English Furniture* (Country Life 1953)
Savage, G.	*Porcelain Through the Ages* (Penguin 1954)
	Pottery Through the Ages (Penguin 1959)
Smith, A.	*Illustrated Guide to Clocks and Watches* (Connoisseur 1975)
Staff, F. W.	*The Picture Postcard and its Origins* (Lutterworth 1966)
Symonds, R. W.	*A History of English Clocks* (Penguin 1947)
Taylor, G.	*Silver* (Penguin 1956)
Toller, J.	*Discovering Antiques* (David & Charles 1975; Newton Abbot)
Vose, R. H.	*Illustrated Guide to Glass* (Connoisseur 1975)
Wakefield, H.	*Nineteenth-Century British Glass* (Faber 1961)
Wills, G.	*Collecting Copper and Brass* (Archer House 1963; New York)
Wood, V.	*Victoriana* (Bell 1960)
Woodhouse, C. B.	*Victoriana Collectors' Handbook* (Bell 1970)

Index

David & Charles have a book on it

Discovering Antiques by Jane Toller tells you where to look, what to look for and how to restore antiques. There are still treasures to be discovered provided the would-be collector knows how to see through their disguises and how to restore items to reveal their original beauty. The knowledge the author provides will make casual strolls through markets and junkshops infinitely more rewarding, for pieces that might so easily be thrown away can be transformed into things of delight and value. Illustrated.

Book Collecting. A Beginner's Guide by Seumas Stewart. Any actual or potential collector of printed books and pamphlets in the English language will enjoy this lively, informative book, whether he seeks fine, rare first editions, or collects books in some particular subject-field. How to start collecting is discussed, and the ways of establishing authenticity; general literature and specialized fields are reviewed, a scale of values allowing the likely cost of acquisitions to be estimated is included, and the full bibliography includes details of the various editions of works by collected authors. Seumas Stewart is himself an antiquarian bookseller. Illustrated.

Antique Cameras by R. C. Smith. This beautifully illustrated book traces the changes in camera design from the early hand-made polished mahogany boxes with their unwieldy tripods to the precision engineering of the Folding Kodak, produced at the beginning of this century. With descriptions of the sliding box and collapsible cameras, apparatus for making stereoscopic pictures, 'detective' and film cameras and many more, it follows too the rise of the new photography, made possible by the chance discovery that ended 40 years of long exposures. Illustrated.

Veteran Sewing Machines by F. Brian Jewell is a collector's guide to old sewing machines whose decorative and practical qualities make them respected mechanical antiques. This first book for collectors describes the fascination of the machines and covers highlights of their development with a directory of marques, details of serial numbers, hints on restoration and a detailed chronology. Illustrated.

Collecting Mechanical Antiques by Ronald Pearsall. The author defines a mechanical antique as a portable implement that does a job of work, as opposed to a scientific instrument, which, like a compass or a telescope, measures or informs. The history and workings of typewriters, sewing machines, phonographs, telephones and many other items are described, many of them cossetted and tortured into artistic shapes by loving Victorian craftsmen, so that it is sometimes difficult to see where science ends and applied art begins. For collectors on a limited budget, there is great scope in this field and many opportunities to make discoveries. Illustrated.

Repairing Antique Clocks: A Guide for Amateurs by Eric P. Smith. Clock-lovers with a talent for practical repairs will welcome this excellent book, written with the amateur collector-cum-repairer in mind. In the author's view, the attraction of old clocks is both aesthetic and mechanical, so both these aspects of horology receive due attention. Illustrated.

Collecting Bookmarkers by A. W. Coysh is the first book devoted solely to a fascinating subject for the collector. Bookmarkers have been in common use for over a century. The earliest were mainly hand-embroidered or painted. In Victorian times they were made from silk and in Edwardian times insurance companies, publishers and booksellers took over with more subtle methods of persuasion. The author has a large collection and many of these are illustrated.

Don't Throw It Away by A. W. Coysh is an entertaining guide to collecting almost every imaginable object from banknotes to valentine cards. Written for the beginner and the amateur enthusiast, the author provides a comprehensively indexed book for easy reference. Illustrated.

128